LEADERS OF THOUGHT

IN THE MODERN CHURCH

BY

REUEN THOMAS

Essay Index Reprint Series

BOOKS FOR LIBRARIES PRESS
FREEPORT, NEW YORK

First Published 1892
Reprinted 1972

Library of Congress Cataloging in Publication Data

Thomas, Reuen, 1840-1907.
Leaders of thought in the modern church.

(Essay index reprint series)
CONTENTS: Jonathan Edwards.--William Ellery
Channing.--John Henry Newman. [etc.]
1. Christian biography. I. Title.
BR1700.T5 1972   209'.2'2 [B]   72-8559
ISBN 0-8369-7333-X

To the Officers
OF
HARVARD CHURCH AND CONGREGATION
WHOSE LOVE AND CONFIDENCE HAVE
BEEN A STIMULUS TO ME DURING
THE YEARS OF MY MINISTRY
IN BROOKLINE
I dedicate this book

PREFATORY NOTE.

THE critical reader will discover that these Essays bear internal evidence of having once been discourses addressed to an audience. That fact accounts for their style being what it is, and for the inweaving into their texture of personal experiences, which characteristics might not be so legitimate if they were literary essays pure and simple.

REUEN THOMAS.

Harvard Church, BROOKLINE,
June, 1892.

CONTENTS.

LEADERS OF THOUGHT

IN THE MODERN CHURCH

I.

JONATHAN EDWARDS.

THAT Jonathan Edwards was the most celebrated of American metaphysicians and divines which the eighteenth century produced, is admitted everywhere. He was born at East Windsor, Conn., October 5, 1703, and lived in this world till 1758. His father was a clergyman, the Rev. Timothy Edwards. His mother was the daughter of a clergyman. He had ten sisters to keep him in good spirits in his dejected hours — probably to torment the life out of him at all hours. He must have been mentally precocious, for as early as

his eighth or ninth year we find him debating
with himself about certain doctrines of the
Christian religion. In his sixteenth year he
had made himself acquainted with one of the
masterly books of the world, " Locke on the
Understanding." This book awoke his mind
in a remarkable degree, and started him on the
road along which he afterward traveled as a
leader — the road of abstract thought. I hope
that the word "metaphysician" will not
frighten you, though it is a word which applies more closely to Jonathan Edwards than
to any other American mind. I am not about
to make any attempt to enter into the subtle-
ties and profundities of his thinking. But as
more than any other man he stands as the representative of the New England of the past, if
not of the present, it will be fitting that we
should try to get a glimpse or two into the internal man before we have done with him.

As to the facts of his life, these may be re-
called. From fourteen years of age to twenty
he was a student at Yale College. He seems
to have received a license to preach at twenty

years of age. His first appointment lasted
only about eight months. He deemed himself
unsuited to it, and retired. For two years he
was tutor in the college at New Haven. He
then received an invitation to be colleague
with his grandfather at Northampton. He
continued in that town for twenty-four years,
and resigned because he could not induce parents to keep bad books out of the hands of
their children ; which bad books, he averred,
hindered the workings of the Spirit of God
among the young. After that he was engaged
by a society which had its headquarters in
London, England, and gave himself to the
preaching of the Gospel to the Housatonic
Indians, at Stockbridge. This simple fact,
that a man of so much eminence that on the
report of his retirement from Northampton he
was immediately invited to go and take up his
residence in Scotland, afterward engaged himself as a missionary to the outcasts of society,
speaks volumes for the meekness of the man.
However, good came out of the evil, as, during
the six years of his missionary work among the

Indians, he devoted his leisure time to those
studies which issued in the book associated
forever with his name, a book which ranks
among the great books of the world — that
on "The Freedom of the Will." This book
was published in 1754. I wonder if any of
you have ever read it. And further, I am
curious to know how many there are among
us who could begin it and hold on to it steadily,
sentence by sentence, and chapter by chapter,
to the end ? There is no milk for babes in that
book, and even men must have first-class mas-
ticating power and a most robust digestion to
appropriate and assimilate such strong meat.
In four years from the time of the publication
of the book, which among thinkers immortal-
ized him, he was offered the presidency of
Princeton College, New Jersey. But he had
scarcely begun his incumbentship before he
died. There was much of that terrible disease
we know by the name of small-pox in the
neighborhood. He submitted to a preventive
treatment, but it took an unfavorable turn in
a constitution doubtless enfeebled by long and

continuous studies, and soon the greatest metaphysician New England has produced ceased from all terrestrial labors. At fifty-five years of age he departed hence.

Not only as a thinker was Jonathan Edwards great, but as a preacher also. It does not by any means follow that a great thinker will necessarily be a great preacher, or even a moderately good preacher. Some men, in the wisdom of divine providence, are intended to be teachers of teachers. Some of us may have had very disappointing experiences in the matter of preaching when it has been done by men whose reputation as thinkers has been of the highest. To have the thought and so to be able to express it as that it shall command the attention and interest the feelings of a general assembly is a combination of endowments very rare to find. The following estimate of him as an orator is supposably correct: " As an orator he sometimes held not only the feelings but the intellects of his hearers completely under his sway. The extraordinary influence which he thus exercised was not due

to any personal advantages; for even when his
oratory was most effective the 'contemptible-
ness of his speech and demeanor' still remained, although it was no longer felt by his
hearers; nor to any special excellencies of
style, for though his language conveyed his
meaning without ambiguity, it did so not only
without any of that peculiar felicity of ar-
rangement which is usually one of the chief
elements of successful oratory, but in a bald,
even in a lumbering and awkward manner.
His eloquence was simply 'intense moral earnestness' expressed in the form of what in more
senses than one might be called 'merciless
logic.' His own description of himself, personally, is that he had ' a constitution in many
respects peculiarly unhappy; attended with
flaccid solids — vapid, sizy, and scarce fluids,
and a low tide of spirits, often occasioning a
kind of childish weakness and contemptible-
ness of speech, presence and demeanor.'"
Those who were his contemporaries have de-
scribed him as a powerful and impressive
preacher, somber and even gloomy in his re-

ligious opinions and sentiments, but earnest, unaffected, and nobly conscientious. He seems to have been the author of that method of church work which is characteristic of New England, known as the 'revival' method. Every now and again, generally once a year, special services have been held, called revival services. To secure a revival is that toward which many pastors work. The method seems to have arisen out of a wave of religious enthusiasm which passed over his own parish in 1740–41. It has been remarked, however, that even in the case of one so great as Dr. Edwards there seem to be inevitable dangers attending this high-pressure system. It was but a few years after this great revival that obscene books were so general among the young of his parish that, rather than seem to tolerate them, he retired from his post. Lest it should be inferred by some that, personally, I am not in sympathy with revival methods, let me here say that I trust that I am in sympathy with everything that is real. When a revival is real it is of a nature which indicates that there

is a more than ordinary spiritual power working on the hearts of the people. The very
idea of it is that it is something exceptional.
That being so, it is not something, I take it,
dependent on the will of man. It is not any
thing we can begin or end. If the conditions
are such that the Spirit of the Most High can
work in an exceptional way, let us believe and
rejoice. But to " get up a revival " seems to
me something closely akin to impiety. I have
known what it is to have a whole year of revival. It came of itself, or rather as God
willed it — as the fruit of continuous and, as
I believe, faithful work on behalf of the
church. There was no effort after it, no extra
services; not the first attempt at excitement.
It was a rain from heaven. And the state of
mind it produced was one of humility and tenderness and rejoicing of heart. I should prefer
to name all special services evangelistic services
—services intended specially for bringing influence to bear on those who are outsiders.
Beyond these few remarks I cannot now enter
on this question.

We must devote the rest of our time to try-
ing to form some simple, but for us it may be
sufficient, estimate of the character and mind
of this fountain of New England orthodoxy —
for such, I suppose, we must regard him.
Evidently he was a good deal of a recluse.
He must have been. It was not possible for
a man of such studious habits to be in society
very much. His books were his real companions, and his teaching and preaching, when
we come to analyze it, was a kind of introduction of his companions to the members of his
parish. The greatest of all English preachers
in the latter part of the eighteenth century
was Robert Hall. He was a kind of Dr.
Samuel Johnson in the pulpit. That for sixty
years such a man should have diligently read
and re-read the works of President Edwards,
and have formed of him this judgment —
"Jonathan Edwards unites comprehensiveness
of view with minuteness of investigation beyond any writer I am acquainted with. He
was the greatest of the sons of men. He has
none of the graces of writing, I admit; he was

acquainted with no grace but divine " — such testimony from such a man goes for an immense deal.

Edwards was a severe logician. That must never be forgotten, and especially when one happens upon a sermon like that of his entitled " Sinners in the hands of an angry God." I should think it must be the most terrific sermon that from a Christian pulpit was ever preached. One has said of that sermon: " I think a person of moral sensibility, alone at midnight, reading that awful discourse, would well-nigh go crazy. He would hear the judgment trump, and see the advancing heaven, and the day of doom would begin to mantle him with its shroud."

The most wonderful effect was produced on the audience during its delivery. It is stated that the hearers groaned and shrieked convulsively, and their outcries of distress once drowned the preacher's voice, and compelled him to make a long pause. Some of the audience seized fast hold upon the pillars and braces of the meeting-house, as if that very

moment their sliding feet were precipitating
them into the gulf of perdition; and a fellow-
clergyman sitting at the time in the pulpit
cried out: "Mr. Edwards, Mr. Edwards! Is
not God merciful, too?" Whether in these
days we are better or worse than were the
men and women of those times, I am not com-
petent to affirm, but I feel confident that no
congregation in the vicinity of Boston would
now sit and listen to a sermon so terrific in its
logical might as that most celebrated of all the
sermons of the great Northampton divine. It
may be that we need preaching of that kind,
if only the man could be found capable of giving it, but only a Jonathan Edwards could so
preach; for only a mind of the remorseless,
logical power of his could possibly gather together and keep in line the material which
was necessary to make his applications of his
theme possible. "It was a kind of moral in-
quisition; and sinners were put upon argu-
mentative racks, and beneath screws, and,
with an awful revolution of the great truth
in hand, evenly and steadily screwed down

and crushed." It would seem to most of us
that, with Edwards' views and opinions, it
was next to impossible for him to love God, in
any sense of the word love with which we are
familiar. He had so profound and all-consum-
ing a sense of awe that love was out of the
question. Everything in his theology was
foundationed on the idea of divine sovereignty,
interpreted not as the New Testament war-
rants us in interpreting it, but interpreted
simply as the just ground of government, of
law and of order. Everywhere in this world
there was rebellion, which must be put down
at any cost. Till the rebellion was crushed
out or the rebels were in everlasting fetters,
there was nothing else to be said to them
about Deity than that he was angry with
them every day. His ethical watchword was
" duty." That which it was a man's duty to
do he must do at any cost. Of course such a
view of things would make men stoical and
resolute. It would train up men of will and
of determination. It would create and mold
into form good fighting men, stern, unrelenting

controversialists. It would give us men and women holding to their opinions with a tenacity that was unconquerable. But would it give the New Testament type of Christian? Read Edwards' most famous sermon, and then turn to the opening sentences of the Sermon on the Mount, or read almost anything which fell from our Lord's lips, and I venture the assertion that any man but the most unimpressible must feel how different the spirit of New Testament Christianity from that of the theology of this Titanic soul.

Logician as he was, it would not be difficult to show that Edwards was not consistent with himself. Possibly you may reply, "Who is?" and remind me of what Emerson says: "A foolish consistency is the hobgoblin of little minds," and that "with consistency a great soul has little to do." Certainly no two men could be wider apart than Emerson and Jonathan Edwards. The one was a magnificent logician, the other seems to have scorned logic as if it were the forbidden fruit on the tree of life. If inconsistency be a sign of a great soul, Emerson himself must be crowned. Oftentimes he seems to have ejected his thoughts just as they came, without any, even the slightest, sense of their having any relations — fathers or mothers, sisters, brothers, cousins or aunts. He was the most fastidious soul in all society, and yet as much an anarchist in the region of mind, as the men incarcerated in Chicago in the region of property. In one sense Emerson may be viewed as the natural reaction from Jonathan Edwards. He of Concord collected together any quantity of material out of which to build a house for the soul; he quarried stone; he cut down timber of the very best; he brought into a heap all precious things — gems of rare quality and color — threw them at your feet, and said: "There, build your own house if you can; and if you can't, live out in the cold; it is all you are good for." Edwards laid a foundation, and laboriously built a house — a big, square, roomy, old-fashioned New England mansion, and said: "There, go in and live in it, or stay out and be damned!" You might object that all the windows looked toward the north, that there was next to no sun in the house, and very little warmth; that it was damp and chill, and must be, from the way in which the house was built; but that, he would say, was no fault of his. God made the material, and it was a house adapted to human nature in its present condition. It was of no use to say to him, " Out of the same materials a house may be built with windows looking toward the south, a house full of light and warmth and cheerfulness, and of better design, in which birds will sing and flowers will bloom, and men, women and children can rejoice and be glad." That is exactly what these stern logicians refuse to see — that out of the same materials a much better and more cheerful house can be built; a house more receptive of the cheering and fertilizing sun and air with which God has filled the universe.

Yet, with all the deductions we are obliged to make from the form into which his thought ran, I yet think that Edwards must take rank as the robustest mind New England has pro-

duced. He was a man of sublime courage.
He spoke out his thought regardless of consequences. He proclaimed the absoluteness
of Deity, and asserted that the Sovereign
Creator had not only power but the right to
act as he willed. If only Edwards had made
it clear that the sovereignty of God was the
sovereignty of right over wrong, of love over
hate, of wisdom over folly, what a magnificent
system of thought his would have been! I,
for one, have no objection to Divine Sovereignty. To me the idea is full of comfort and
of hope. I do not object to the idea of absoluteness in the will of Deity when I find from
the lips of the Christ that God's will is my
salvation, that he wills that all men shall be
saved and come to a knowledge of the truth.
To ascribe arbitrariness to Deity is to say that
God acts according to the pattern we have in
men of infirmity and something worse. Edwards seemed to teach that God was simply
a "happy" being, removed from all participa-
tion in the sorrows of his people. The word
"happy" seems to me a weak word. There

are sorrows that arise from imperfection, and there are sorrows that arise from perfection. The quality is different. There is sorrow which is only an element in perfectness. The divine sympathy means in some way the divine sorrow. As one has said, " happy " is an unfortunate and an " epicurean epithet." Edwards could speak of disinterested love to God as something seemingly obtainable by mortals in this state. " Disinterested " love is, of course, love that has no expectation of benefits arising from it ; no dislike of punishment or suffering which comes from the one loved ; it must arise above all mere gratitude, and must love the Being simply for what he is.

When a logician discourses on such a theme, it reveals in his nature immensely more than the logician. Such disinterested love is not, I fear, possible to us of these days ; but when a man begins to speak of such a theme he is beyond all system ; there is something even repellent about systematizing love. The greatest of all great forces is thus outside all our theologic systems. And the conflict of our

own and of all days is to save the systems of
the past and yet to let in the love and light
of God freely upon human spirits. As a
thinker, as a logician, as a metaphysician,
New England has produced no one greater than
Jonathan Edwards. His place was in the
eighteenth century; ours is in the nineteenth.
We admire Edwards, but we bow the knee to
One only — the Teacher of Edwards and of all
others who have been truth-loving and truth-
speaking men.

II.

WILLIAM ELLERY CHANNING.

WILLIAM ELLERY CHANNING lived in this world of ours from 1780 to 1842. His birthplace was Newport, R. I. He owed an immense deal to the ancestry immediately back of him. We are told that from his father he inherited a fine person, simple and elegant tastes, sweetness of temper, and warmth of affection ; from his mother, who seems to have been a woman of more than ordinary endowment, he derived the higher benefits of that strong moral discernment and straightforward rectitude of purpose and action which formed so striking a feature of his character. As in so many cases of men who have had high character and great influence,

his mother's training of him was constant and
unremitting, exercised with a judgment and
discrimination that in itself amounted almost
to genius. Aside from his mother, he seems
to have been indebted to the character of persons in lowly positions for some of the best
influences which operated on his life. An invalid woman; a cooper who refused, though
very poor, to manufacture articles used in his
trade for containing ardent spirits; a female
servant who illustrated before his eyes the
cheerfulness which true piety could bring with
it — these were the influences which operated
on his youthful temperament, and gave him
views of people which remained with him all
through life; gave him, too, the interest he
always had in the slave, the poor, and the
sick.

We have, in these brief lectures, to do with
men as thinkers, and so with Channing in that
capacity. A man may be of great influence in
his day, and yet not be characteristically a
thinker. Channing was a man of large benevolence, and in that capacity is a most inter-

esting character. But as a thinker how did he
stand ? Had he independence enough to be a
thinker; independence enough to retain possession of himself and of his speech so as to
tell to others with sincerity and truth that
which he saw and heard in the temple of
truth ? It is evident that he had the independence necessary. Had he the power of
vision which is necessary to the thinker — the
power to look into a thing as well as at it ?
Had he that spiritual discernment which looks
through phenomena into the essential heart of
things ? Had he that dissatisfaction with out-
sides which compels a man to push inwardly
and still inwardly until his mind finds some
permanent ground for that he holds as truth ?
These questions cannot be answered with a
simple "yes" or "no." At the end of this
lecture we may answer them more intelligently
than at this stage in our inquiry.

Perhaps this is the proper place to ask
whether a minister has any right to do his
own thinking — if he can — or whether he has
simply to accept what men in other genera-

tions have said as sufficient, and sink himself
in them ? Some of you will be astonished to
hear such a question, but it is certainly as-
sumed by some that thinking is no part of a
minister's duty. His duty is piously to accept
what others have thought, without asserting
any individuality of his own. " Your remark
applies to the Church of Rome," some one is
inclined to say. It applies elsewhere. It applies to Protestant churches. There are many
inconsistent Romanists, but on all points on
which the Church has given a deliverance a
consistent Romanist ceases from thinking.
He has no liberty in regard to that on which
the Church has given a dogmatic deliverance.
He gives up his conscience and his intelligence
into the keeping of the Church. But are we
to do that, or anything like it in our Protestant
churches ? Protestantism, as I understand it,
claims for Jesus Christ and his moral and
spiritual sovereignty over men that which
Romanism claims for the Church and the Pope.
We claim infallibility for Jesus Christ. Romanists claim infallibility for the Pope and

the Church as speaking through an Œcumeni-
cal Council. Is it not easy to see that any
church which claims infallibility or finality
for its standard is not Protestant but Papal —
whatever name it bears ? A Protestant church
has this as its controlling principle: "Holy
Scripture contains all things necessary to salvation, so that whatsoever is not read therein,
or may be proved thereby, is not to be required
of any man as necessary to salvation." Now,
if any minister is simply to be a receiver of
other men's thoughts — is not himself a thinker
— is not he forfeiting something that God has
given him ? Is he not putting an authority
between himself and God — an authority for
which there is no authority ? Use all helps,
certainly; get all the help you can out of
other men whom God has largely endowed;
but if I have any ability to be a thinker, I am
of the conviction that my duty to God demands that I use that ability. Have I not
the same right to examine the original Scriptures for myself that another man has, that
other men in other generations had ? If any

man has a right that does not belong to me,
I want to see his credentials. Who gave another man a right to set himself up as a
standard? And if no one man has the right,
have any number of ones the right? If I do
not go, supposing I can get there, to Jesus
Christ himself, if I do not listen to his words,
examine his deeds, put myself in as close pro-
pinquity to him as I am able; if I, believing
the Scriptures were given through men so inspired as to be channels of divine truth, do
not search those Scriptures, if I let another
man search them for me and then accept him
or any number of men as final — I, for my
part, cannot perceive how I am accepting my
Lord's command to come direct to him and
find rest to my soul; nor can I perceive
wherein I stand on any other ground than
that on which the Romanist stands: some
Pope or some papal hierarchy stands between
me and God's Christ and the Scriptures which
contain and unfold him to my perception.
Duty to Christ seems to me to demand that I
give him a full and fair opportunity so to

operate on my mind as that he can get all the truth into it of which it is capable. If I allow another man to come between me and him as an infallible authority, my allegiance is compound and not simple. If a man comes between me and Christ as a pair of spectacles comes between short sight and the things seen, making it clear, that is the true helpful relation ; but if a man comes between me and God's Christ and stops me short at himself, he is an intruder. If he will not get out of the way I have a perfect right to run over him, even though he should say that it is a very heterodox proceeding. Now, in this sense that he who has independence enough, earnestness enough, sincerity enough, to think for himself is a thinker, Channing was a thinker, and has a right to be classed among the thinkers of the modern church. If a thinker is always a man of great reverence, with the spirit of investigation so developed in him that he is incessantly laborious in his perseverance, then Channing was a thinker. But he was not a profound thinker. The limit to his ability as

a thinker was soon reached. He laboriously
trained himself to "the mastery of that copious and vigorous style of composition to which
his subsequent position in the world of letters
is in no small measure due." His laborious
culture of his mind seems to have kept him in
that enfeebled condition of body which was
chronic with him.

His sense of responsibility was almost op-
pressive, and he wrought with such full putting forth of his powers that everything of
his seems to glow and burn with life. Though
he takes rank with the Unitarians, yet I am
informed that he would have much preferred
not to identify himself with any theological
party. It is a pretty hard thing for a man on
whom is a party name to be held accountable
for everything said and done by men bearing
the same badge. Because, as a rule, every denomination is "run" — to use a word which is
more popular than classical — by its smallest
men; men who are very fond of place and
office; good men who are not great men, and,
as one says, "Goodness which is not greatness

also is a sad misfortune "; it is, when it gets
into any place of leadership. How often we
hear the remark as an apologetic for some act
which is as faulty in judgment and as bad in
spirit as it well can be, " But So-and-so is such
a good man!" A small, good man, with an
obstinate conscience, in a place of influence
can do more harm in a few years than can
be rectified in a lifetime. When talking of
"goodness" I am inclined often to say, "There
is none good save one, Jesus Christ." Observe
how all his goodness was greatness too. Con-
scientiousness is not the whole of Christianity; it is a very small part of it. A very
small man all conscience is a hedgehog — all
spikes. My conviction is that St. Paul knew
what he was talking about when he put that
most human and divine thing, " love," above
everything, and said that, practically, without
it a man was not of much account. Now, when
Channing, with great reverence for such men
as Dr. Hopkins and Dr. Stiles, could not
follow them, but must study the character of
Christ and the Scriptures for himself, and act

and preach according to his individuality, he
was largely moved to it by the emphasis which
he found everywhere in Scripture on love of
the brotherhood — God's love for man, God
sending Jesus Christ to seek and to save man.
Scripture did not put its great emphasis on
this, "Be conscientious," but "Be Christian,
love God and love man because he is God's
man, and great shall your reward in Heaven
be." Channing never seems to have pene-
trated into what we may call the metaphysics
of theology. The doctrine of a Trinity in the
divine nature was beyond him; the why and
wherefore of an atonement he could not undertake to affirm; and so he confined himself
pretty much to such expressions as these:
"The blood of Christ was shed for souls;"
"The Son of God himself left the abodes of
glory and expired a victim on the cross."
Always and everywhere he seemed to worship
Jesus the Christ as the unique Son of God,
and to be entranced by the practical benevolence of his life, by his self-sacrifice, by his
disinterested offering of himself on the altar,

a victim for man; but very seldom do you
find him wrestling in the great deeps of theologic thought, like Edwards, or like that most
fascinating of all modern writers on the Atonement — John McLeod Campbell. Channing
believed in Christ's pre-existence, and that he
came down from Heaven for man's salvation,
and he taught "that the Scriptures ascribe
the remission of sins to Christ's death with an
emphasis so peculiar that we ought to consider
this event as having a special influence in re-
moving punishment — as a condition or method
of pardon, without which repentance would
not avail us, at least to that extent which is
now promised by the Gospel." This is mar-
velously near to being a correct setting forth
of vicariousness in the sacrifice our Lord made
of himself. Channing seems to have been a
man who wanted to take what commended itself to him as truth wherever he found it, at
the same time to keep on the working side of
all truth — the practical, benevolent, hospita-
ble side. There is no little wisdom in that
attitude. "I wish," he said in one of his ser-

mons, "to regard myself as belonging, not to
a sect, but to the community of free minds, of
lovers of truth, and followers of Christ both
in Heaven and on earth — to stand under the
open sky in the broad light, looking far and
wide, seeing with my own eyes, hearing with
my own ears, and following Truth meekly but
resolutely, however arduous or solitary be the
path in which she leads."

And so it has come to pass that all truth-
seeking men have been interested in Channing.
Let us take only one testimony, and that from
one of the most gifted men of modern times —
I mean the late Rev. F. W. Robertson. In
letter No. 55, in his biography, we find these
words :

" Dr. Channing's life is full of interest. He
had no adventures ; nor were his inward strug-
gles, as detailed at least, very striking. He
had taken immense pains with himself ; but
the nobler element of his nature was so
strongly predominant that his life was steady,
continuous victory. The purest love for man,
the most unconquerable trust in human nature,

seem to have been the very basis of his being. He was a Unitarian ; but that is a very wide term, including a vast variety of persons thinking very differently on essentials. I can only say that I should be very glad if, half of those who recognize the hereditary claims of the Son of God to worship bowed down before his moral dignity with an adoration half as profound, or a love half as enthusiastic, as Dr. Channing's. I wish I, a Trinitarian, loved and adored him, and the divine goodness in him, anything near the way in which Channing felt. A religious lady found the book on my table, the other day, and was horror-struck. I told her that if she and I ever got to Heaven, we should find Dr. Channing revolving around the central Light, in an orbit immeasurably nearer than ours, almost invisible to us, and lost in a blaze of light."

Many other testimonies of this kind might be adduced from men of great spiritual insight who had no denominational affinities with Dr. Channing. To me it seems that the defect in Dr. Channing's teaching arose from

the fact that he had all his life long been with
people who illustrated human nature on a much
higher level than the average. Consequently
he had no adequate views of the malignity
there is in sin, and of the fearful wreck it
makes of all that is human in this nature of
ours. If he had been a missionary abroad, or
even a city missionary at home in some of the
worst parts of our great cities, and had seen,
again and again, the moral, spiritual and
physical wrecks which are everywhere to be
met there, he would have spoken differently
about human nature under the power of sin.
Christ Jesus would have been, if possible,
more necessary to him than he was. He would
have realized more completely than was possible to him, with his experience, the need of
regeneration, and not simply reformation, for
man. Reform and renewal are words expressing differences that stretch to the roots of
things. Channing was a great philanthropist,
a great patriot, great in other departments,
but I should not say that his thinking went to
the roots of things. He moved in the sphere

of that which was benevolent, practical, and immediately useful. In that region his influence was immense. He was much like one for whom I have great admiration because of the purity and beauty of his character — Dr. A. P. Peabody. He seems to me almost the only living representative of the Channing type of New England clergy. The late Dr. Sears, author of that most instructive volume, " The Fourth Gospel, the Heart of Christ," was another of the order. Perhaps the Rev. James Freeman Clarke approaches as near to the spirit of Channing as any modern man outside these. I should perhaps be more accurate if I were to say that could this eminent man and another man almost equally eminent — the Rev. Edward Everett Hale — be rolled into one, you would have Channing. It is not for me, however, to judge living men. I only give my impression. It seems to me that if Unitarianism had continued on the high elevation which it maintained in Channing, it would have had a different kind of influence from that which it has exerted. But I do not wish to invite

controversy. I could wish that we all were as
clear-sighted on some matters as was Channing. For myself, I confess to having great
delight in his writings. They animate and in-
spire me. That the practical nature of the
man may be evident, and as an illustration of
the wise discrimination he makes, let us take
one or two extracts from an address of his on
Temperance. He includes other things besides
those to which this word strictly applies. For
instance, speaking of dancing, he has no objection to it as a recreation conducted under
the laws of gymnastics. But when he comes
to speak of the ball-room he writes: "The
time consumed in preparation for a ball, the
waste of thought upon it, the extravagance of
dress, the late hours, the exhaustion of
strength, the exposure of health, and the lan-
guor of the succeeding day — these and other
evils are strong reasons for banishing it from
the community." Then again he writes: "I
approach another subject on which a greater
variety of opinion exists than on the last, and
that is the theater. In its present state the

theater deserves no encouragement. It is an
accumulation of immoral influences. It has
nourished intemperance and all vice. I can
conceive of a theater which would be the noblest of all forms of amusements, and would
take rank among the means of refining the
taste and elevating the character of the people " (but he owns that it does not exist).
Then he adds, taking facts as they are : " Is it
possible that a Christian and a refined people
can resort to theaters where exhibitions of
dancing are given fit only for brothels, and
where the most licentious class in the community throng. unconcealed, to tempt and to
destroy ? That the theater should be suffered
to exist in its present degradation is a reproach
to the community. In the meantime (he asks)
is there not an amusement having an affinity
with the drama, which might be usefully introduced among us ? I mean recitation. A
work of genius recited by a man of fine taste,
enthusiasm, and powers of elocution, is a very
pure and high gratification. Shakespeare
worthily recited would be better understood

than on the stage. Then, in recitation we escape the weariness of listening to poor performers, who, after all, fill up most of the time at the theater."

And so, with just judgment and rare discrimination, he goes on to separate between the instructive and destructive. In our day people swallow anything and everything under the perverted and senseless idea of freedom. Cannot a man let alone indigestible things, and offal and garbage, and still be free ? Is he not exercising his freedom more by letting some things alone than by insanely appropriating them simply because he may ? The way in which some addle-pated people talk about freedom is enough to make the word disreputable. There is something necessary to life besides freedom — viz., intelligence, the trained ability to discriminate, the strength to refuse as well as to accept. On such practical matters as these to which I have referred, Channing is a most wholesome teacher and guide. His words have a tonic quality in them which we all sorely need. Take an admirable address

of his on the Elevation of the Working Classes.
I wish ,that every workingman in the land
could be induced to read it and re-read it until
it had become like a dose of iron in his blood.
In my copy I find every third or fourth sentence marked as excellent. He speaks of elevation of soul as the only true elevation of
man or woman anywhere. " That idleness is a
privilege and work a disgrace," he says, " is
among the deadliest of errors. Without depth
of thought, or earnestness of feeling, or
strength of purpose, living an unreal life, sacrificing substance to show, substituting the
factitious for the natural, mistaking a crowd
for society, finding its chief pleasure in ridi-
cule, and exhausting its ingenuity in expe-
dients for killing time — fashion is among the
last influences under which a human being
who respects himself, or who comprehends the
great end of life, would desire to be placed."
If these words were necessary in Channing's
day, how much more in ours ! " Labor," he
says, " is a far better condition for the reception of great ideas than luxurious or fashion-

able life." "There is no elevation without moral and religious principle." "What avails intellectual without moral power?" All that is benevolent and practical in Channing's teaching is most admirable in quality. He thinks clearly and speaks with great precision and power in this region. It is only when he approaches the region of pure thought — that region in which Jonathan Edwards was so great a master — that he falters. He is one of those men who belong to us all. There are some men, let them have on them this badge or that, you cannot denominationalize them. They are too great to be ismatics or schismatics. They draw all kinds and orders of men to them. Men see the light in them; they take knowledge of them that they have been with Jesus. I am speaking to you principally of men of this order. Channing was one of them. He had an eye to discern wherein the strength and weakness of men and nations lay. Whosoever is incapable of admiring the simple and Christian manfulness of Channing must be in a bad moral state. At a time when it was a fashionable thing to exalt France because of the heroic conduct of a single Frenchman, he warned his nation against the fatal influence of French morals and manners. He dreaded above all things an alliance of these United States with France. And when it was thought to be the patriotic thing to sow the seeds of distrust against England, he as manfully uttered these words, showing a discernment which has so generally been lacking as to the class of society in which the real, typical Englishman is to be found: "The character of England is to be estimated particularly from what may be called the middle class of society, the most numerous class in all nations, and more numerous and influential in England than in any other nation of Europe.

"The warm piety, the active benevolence, and the independent and manly thinking which are found in this class, do encourage me in the belief that England will not be forsaken by God in her solemn struggle. I feel myself bound to all nations by the ties of

a common nature, a common Father, and a
common Saviour. But I feel a particular interest in England, for I believe that there
Christianity is exerting its best influence on
the human character; that there the perfec-
tions of human nature, wisdom, virtue, and
piety are fostered by excellent institutions, and
are producing the delightful fruits of domestic
happiness, social order, and general prosperity.
It is a hope which I could not resign without
anguish, that the 'prayers and alms' of England will 'come up for a memorial before God,'
and will obtain for her his sure protection
against the common enemy of the civilized
world."

These are brave as well as good words.
They show us how Channing was more dis-
cerning, greater and braver than most of the
men of his time. While, for myself, I cannot
stop where he stops in his thinking on the
highest and subtlest themes of theology, yet I
cannot withhold from him on that account my
poor, but sincere tribute of admiration and
gratitude for all that he was and did and spake.

Before we have finished this brief course of lectures we shall encounter men who as thinkers were much profounder and greater than Channing; but, take him for all in all, he was a great and beautiful soul, in the truest sense, one of God's elect.

III.

JOHN HENRY NEWMAN.

IN making a selection from many names in the hemisphere of the modern church, I have tried to select such as stand for different phases of thought and action; or, as we might say, the heads of different schools of thought. John Henry Newman is the most respectable and most interesting name in that school which is known as the Oxford School, because it had its rise in the English University of Oxford. Pusey, Keble, Hurrell Froude, H. J. Rose, Oakley, and others were its leaders. The names of Newman and Pusey are the best known, and these two men were most influential of all those who, though members of a church professedly Protestant, yet steadily

fought against everything characteristically
Protestant in it until they succeeded to no
inconsiderable extent in persuading very many
of its ministry and people to discard the name
of Protestant altogether. The "movement"
was known for a while as Puseyism, although
Dr. Pusey as to influence was second to Newman; but the name of Newman was so easily
elongated by a syllable which travestied it that
no one dared to call the movement Newman-
ism because it was clear that its opponents
would call it Newmanianism. Then it became
known as Ritualism, and as Anglo-Catholicism.
From the first it was a movement toward
Rome, and if it continued to move there was no
logical stopping-place short of Rome. John
Henry Newman represented the spirit and
the logical consistency of the movement more
honestly and thoroughly than any other man.
The question has often been asked, "How do
you explain it that a man like Newman should
become a Romanist; a man of so much culture
and intelligence and ability?" He has himself answered that question in the most inter-

esting book he ever wrote — a book which would possibly never have been written but for an attack upon his honesty and straightforwardness, made by the Rev. Charles Kingsley. It was hardly possible, in the absence of any explanation of himself, for a man like Mr. Kingsley to understand the order of mind which belonged to Newman. Kingsley was not characteristically a theologian, nor very much of an ecclesiastic. He was a manly man, who took the most charitable and common-sense view of every subject, and tried, in a simple, manly fashion, to serve God and his fellow-man. To him Newman seemed so subtle and so evasive that the impression on Kingsley's mind was that such a man could not be true and honest. He might be an exquisite writer of English prose, a man of much personal magnetism, and very devout ecclesiastically ; but how can such a man be transparently honest and straightforward ? Newman's " Apologia " is an answer to Kingsley's question — a very elaborate and, in one sense, an all-sufficient answer.

Newman was born in London in 1801. Until the year 1845 he was a minister in the Episcopal Church of England. In that year he united himself with the Church of Rome. Only a few years since he was made a cardinal in that church. Some thirty-five volumes, chiefly on ecclesiastical and theological themes, have, in the course of his long life, been published of his authorship. He has a brother four years younger than himself who moved as rapidly as himself, only in the other direction. This brother, Francis William Newman, is an Oxford man, too, and was more of a scholar at college than John Henry, obtaining what is known as a double first class — first class in classics and first class in mathematics. When it came to taking his degree he declined to sign the Thirty-nine Articles of the Church of England, resigned his fellowship, and withdrew from the University. This brother was afterward appointed classical tutor in Bristol College, then in Manchester New College, and finally, in 1846, his reputation for scholarship led to his being appointed to the Latin chair in Uni-

versity College, London, which he held till
1863. He is the author of some twenty
volumes on different themes, all showing accurate scholarship and great thinking power.
It is seldom that one and the same mother
has two such sons as John Henry and Francis
William Newman — both starting from the
same place and moving in exactly opposite
directions; one becoming an advocate of the
extreme rationalistic school, the other of the
extreme dogmatical school. The same home
and college influences operating on the minds
of two brothers moving them in precisely opposite directions! Such is the mystery of life.

When we take John Henry Newman's account of himself we are saved from the danger
of doing him injustice. The evidence is all
in, and it is his own. From the beginning of
his revelations of himself we cannot refuse to
recognize that he was naturally superstitious.
That remark may to a degree be true of us all.
When people refuse to sit thirteen at table, or
are affrighted at spilling salt, or refuse to turn
a cat away from the house simply because it

is black, it is beyond question that something of superstition abides in such natures. Newman writes of himself: "I was very superstitious, and for some time previous to my conversion (when I was fifteen) used constantly to cross myself on going into the dark." He did not know where he got this practice. His imagination as a boy, he tells us, ran on unknown influences, on magical powers, on talismans. When he was ten years of age he began to write verses. He had a copy-book on the first page of which in schoolboy hand he wrote, "John H. Newman, February 11, 1811. Verse Book." Between "Verse" and "Book" he tells us he had drawn the figure of a solid cross upright, and next to it is what may indeed be meant for a necklace, but what I cannot make out to be anything else than a set of beads suspended with a little cross attached. The strange thing is, he adds, "how, among the thousand things which meet a boy's eyes, these in particular should so have fixed themselves in my mind that I made them thus practically my own."

He speaks of these things as if there was a
kind of predestination in them — as if they
were indications to him of the way he was
bound to go. This book "Apologia" was
written, you will remember, long after he
became a Romanist, and as tracing the order
of ideas and feelings in him from the first.
If these records have anything to teach us, it
is surely this: that the earliest impressions
made on sensitive and susceptible minds are
as seeds out of which the future will grow,
and that whatever appeals to the eye in childhood is likely to have a more lasting influence
than that which appeals to the ear. "When
I was fifteen a great change of thought took
place in me. I fell under the influence of a
definite creed, and received into my intellect
impressions of dogma which, through God's
mercy, have never been effaced or obscured."
He says in later life that he is still as sure of
his conversion at fifteen as he was of his
hands and feet. It is not necessary for our
purpose to trace out step by step the progress
of development in this man's life. He is a

thinker only to this extent, that he impressed himself so powerfully upon the young men of his time while he was at Oxford, and made them in large numbers see as he saw and feel as he felt.

His nature was very superstitious, to begin with. Then he had great imagination, which would be affected by that which was impressive and mystical in religious services and buildings and ecclesiastical hierarchies and orders. But, strange to say, along with this exuberant imaginativeness there was, even more than he himself seems to have had any idea of, but which his critics have all recognized, a logical faculty of exceptional strength, which would compel him, if he meant to have any comfort out of himself, to follow his premises to their inevitable conclusions, wherever they led him. Then, also, his mind was subtle to such a degree that if he had been a lawyer he would, if he had wished to do it, have mystified almost any jury. This charge of subtlety borders so closely on the capacity for skillful Jesuitism that I should decline to make it if it were simply an inference of my own, even though I held it most honestly.

You shall judge for yourself by a single extract from his writings. He is speaking of the Thirty-nine Articles of the Episcopal Church of England, which, as a minister, he had signed. Nine out of every ten persons reading those Articles would affirm that there was no doubt of their evangelical, if not strictly Calvinistic character. It is evident that Newman, as he grows more and more to hate Luther and the Reformation, yet wants to retain his place in the Church of England, has much trouble as to his consistency on account of these articles of belief. After grappling with them over and over again, he is finally impressed with their vagueness and indecisiveness. Then he gets a step further, and writes: "The Articles are evidently framed on the principle of leaving open large questions on which the controversy hinges. They state broadly extreme truths, and are silent about their adjustment. For instance, they say that all necessary faith must be proved

from Scripture, but they do not say who is
to prove it. They say that the Church has
authority in controversies; they do not say
what authority. They say that men are law-
fully called, and sent to minister and preach,
who are chosen and called by men who have
public authority given them in the congregation; but they do not add by whom the
authority is to be given. They say councils
called by princes may err; they do not deter-
mine whether councils called in the name of
Christ may err."

Now, what are we to think of this kind of
argumentation? I should say — if I did not
know whose words these were — that such
argumentation indicated a man who had an
end to gain, and meant to gain it by some
means. This kind of argumentation would
suggest, in any man but John Henry Newman,
smartness, but scarcely honesty. What I mean
is, that this is not an honest use of those
Thirty-nine Articles. Supposing we should
apply the same method to the ten commands
of the moral law: "The Sixth Commandment

says, 'Thou shalt not kill'; but it does not
say thou shalt not make a pit in front of a
little babe toddling about a garden, so that it
may fall in and break its neck. The Eighth
Commandment says, 'Thou shalt not steal';
but it does not say, 'Thou shalt not pay thy-
self that which thou honestly thinkest ought
to come to thee out of thy employer's money.'
And as none of the Commandments say, 'Thou
shalt not get drunk,' it leaves the matter an
open question."

There is an evident viciousness in this mode
of argument which (I do not say in this case)
would ordinarily indicate a mind capable of
deceiving itself. No mode of argument in the
ecclesiastical and theological region is fair and
honest which cannot be applied with good
results in the commercial and moral regions.
I do not wonder that a man like Charles
Kingsley should have had serious doubts as
to Newman's perfect honesty. Supposing
the anarchists in Chicago should take their
stand on this plea: "The Constitution of the
State of Illinois says, 'Thou shalt do no mur-

der,' but it does not say, 'Thou shalt not use
dynamite when in the presence of a police-
man.' " I see no difference radically and
essentially between Dr. Newman's method of
treating the Thirty-nine Articles and the anarchists' method of treating the Constitution
of the State of Illinois. I think I have said
enough to warrant my affirmation that Dr.
Newman had a mind of most marvelous subtlety. As our limits are soon reached, I must
not forget the question which has been asked,
" How do you account for it that a man like
Dr. Newman could go into the Church of
Rome ? " To answer this question we must
recognize, not only the man's natural mental
state, but also that he belonged, to begin with,
to an exclusive church ; that he was born in it
and nurtured in it; also that he was educated
at the most exclusive of all universities, where
even laymen who would take the ordinary
degrees in arts had to profess allegiance to
this church. He did not start from Biblicalism or pure Protestantism. His logical mind
would necessarily ask, Why this exclusiveness

in my church? It can only be justified on
the ground of its being the one and only true
church. Is it? Then would come inquiry
into its history — diligent search, as we know
there was. The results of that diligent search
are given step by step in the " Apologia." I
am minister of an exclusive church. This
exclusiveness means that there is but one true
church. Is my church the one true church?
Let me see. Then went on from day to day
the process of search — from day to day, from
year to year — until, in 1841, we find him
writing in this wise: " Such acts were in
progress (within my church, *i. e.*) as led to the
gravest suspicion, not that it would soon cease
to be a church, but that, since the sixteenth
century, it had never been a church all along."
After that point was reached there was constant struggle with himself to avoid the inevitable conclusion that with his views and
opinions he would have to go elsewhere.

Eventually he went into that church toward
which for years he had been gravitating. Every
step he had taken for years had been a step

nearer to it. The more I examine into Dr.
Newman's views and opinions, the more clearly
I recognize his mental composition, his natural superstitions, his extreme sensitiveness to
everything which appealed to his imagination,
his mystic reverence for everything which was
impressive in services and orders, his subtlety
of mind which could always find a way out of
a difficulty when it presented itself, and which
enabled him to say on one occasion, in giving
an account of himself, " I was not unwilling to
insinuate truths into our church which I thought
had a right there." When added to this I
find in him a faculty seldom associated with
these traits to which I have referred — the
logical faculty — I do not wonder that John
Henry Newman found himself eventually in
the Church of Rome ; my only wonder is that
scores of others did not go with him. With
all that has been said about the refinement of
Newman's nature, there was an intolerance in
it which sometimes broke out into very ugly
forms of expression; as when, for instance, in
some reference to the great Dr. Arnold of

Rugby, he asked snappishly, "But was Arnold
a Christian?" Such a question shocks and
startles one. It forces us to demand from
such a man his definition of a Christian.
What is a Christian? A man who trusts and
loves the Lord Jesus Christ — or what? Newman and his school did not believe for a moment that men had a right to come to the
Scriptures of truth and search them for themselves, prayerfully and diligently, taking them
as they stand. He and they seemed to have
thought more of "the Fathers" and their interpretation than of aught else. Principal Tulloch has remarked upon the total want of the
"historic spirit" in the members of this school.
"The Fathers" were taken without question.
A heap of documents of varying authority, or of
no authority, were put before the reader. The
Ignatian Epistles passed unchallenged (most
of them are regarded as spurious) and, in one
way and another, play a significant part in the
controversy. If a writing contained the assertion of what were called "Church Principles,"
this was ample guarantee of its excellence and

genuineness. "No movement ever started with a larger begging of the question."

It may well be asked, How could Dr. Newman accept the Romish miracles such as the liquefaction of the blood of St. Januarius, and such (to us) absurdities ? Well, I positively do not know, save that, having accepted the dogma of the infallibility of the Church of Rome to begin with, everything else follows as a matter of course. He recognizes and argues for the correctness of all these Romish miracles on the principle that there were miracles in our Lord's time, and therefore may be and are likely to be again. It is a mystery to me that Dr. Newman cannot perceive that the miracles of our Lord's time were all miracles of revelation — they all bring into most impressive form some great truth. These Romish miracles are mere puppet-show work by the side of them. Having spent the greater part of a week studying Dr. Newman's "Apologia" and other productions of his, to try if I can really get some fresh light on this man and his mental history, I am obliged

to acknowledge that to me there is something
sad and discouraging in the revelation of so
accomplished a man swallowing everything
which he finds in " the Fathers " as if it were
more authoritative than the Gospel itself.
He seems to start out with this premise: there
is a visible and infallible Catholic Church
somewhere — where is it ? Eventually he is
certain that his own church is not it, and there
is no other church but the Church of Rome
which can be it. Where did his own church
get the idea of its ministers being sacrificing
priests ? From the Church of Rome. Where
did it get its idea of the eucharist, of baptismal
regeneration, of apostolic succession ? From
the Church of Rome. It must, then, be a
branch of this same church. But why secede
from the mother church ? Was not such
secession schism ? Then he began to hate
Luther ; the very name Protestantism became
odious to him. His intensely logical mind
carried him into the only consistent position
for one holding his views. Those who did not
go with him were in a logically untenable posi-

tion. Newman alone, of all the leaders of the movement, followed out his premises to their conclusions.

How do we know that his views and opinions are not true ? We know it because his views and opinions are not large enough to be true. There is a larger idea of catholicity than his, a larger idea of priesthood, a larger idea of the Church. The New Testament teaches that all who love our Lord Jesus Christ in sincerity belong to the catholic Church, part of which is in heaven and part on earth; it teaches that all believers are priests unto God ; it teaches that every true disciple of Christ belongs to the Church of Christ. These ideas are larger, wider, grander, more comprehensive than those of Newman, undeniably Scriptural, and so true. Only by receiving, by personally appropriating the larger truth can we be saved from the temptation to substitute something inferior for it. Concerning the book that Newman wrote on the eve of his reception into the Roman communion, " The Theory of Development," a book intended to be the explanation and justification of his course, one of the most accomplished and profound of English theologians wrote to a friend: " I am surprised at X's wishing you to read Newman's book. It is a very able book, and one which is likely to produce an effect upon young men. . . . But of all books I ever read, it seems to me the most skeptical; much more calculated to make skeptics than Romanists, though probably it will make some of each class. The trouble is that we have not been setting God before us; that we have been seeking ourselves in our religion and in everything else. This system of Newman's, though to those brought up in it, it may be identified with all that is most holy and godly, will to us be a refuge from God, a more entire, hopeless pursuit of selfish objects. They want the living God, and they fly to the fiction of ecclesiastical authority; they want to be delivered from the burden of self, and they run to the confessor, who will keep them in an eternal round of contrivances to extinguish self by feeding it and thinking of it. To go anywhere for the sake of comfortable

feelings is a deep delusion; to go anywhere
for the sake of truth is the greatest of all
duties. I rose up from the book with a feeling of sadness and depression, as if I were in
the midst of a country under a visitation of
locusts." We can often enter into spiritual
sympathy with men with whom we can have
no intelligent or conscientious ecclesiastical
affinity. In the progress of inward development souls often come into lonely places, into
conditions of inward experience where each
has to bear his own burden. At such times
there is scarcely a hymn to be found more
tenderly expressive than that of Newman's :

> " Lead, kindly Light, amid th' encircling gloom,
>   Lead thou me on;
> The night is dark, and I am far from home,
>   Lead thou me on.
> Keep thou my feet; I do not ask to see
> The distant scene; one step enough for me.
>
> " I was not ever thus, nor pray'd that thou
>   Shouldst lead me on;
> I loved to choose and see my path; but now
>   Lead thou me on.
> I loved the garish day; and, spite of fears,
> Pride ruled my will: remember not past years.

" So long thy power has blest me, sure it still
    Will lead me on
O'er moor and fen, o'er crag and torrent, till
    The night is gone,
And with the morn, those angel faces smile
Which I have loved long since and lost awhile."

IV.

THOMAS CHALMERS.

SCOTTISH Presbyterianism has produced no man of the celebrity of Dr. Chalmers. Edward Irving was a more picturesque man — a man who, to the poet, would be more fascinating, a better subject for a poem or a novel than Chalmers. Mrs. Oliphant has given us a most captivating life of this, as Carlyle calls him, "the most brotherly of men" — for a time the assistant of Chalmers. What a unique thing it must have been to see these two mighty men together — one so richly endowed with vision and imagination, soaring away in the clouds in search of his Lord whom he fain would compel to come down to earth again ; the other a many-sided man, a man of great-

nesses so many and varied that a quotation
from Sydney Smith might well apply to him
— "He was not one man, he was a thousand
men." Thomas Chalmers was born in 1780,
and lived in this world till 1847. From the
first he was a student, and somewhat precocious too, for he entered the University of
St. Andrew's while only eleven years old.
These Scottish universities, however, were at
that time very little more than superior gram-
mar schools, and Scottish boys could study
hard without being greatly injured by it, having too much bone and muscle to be nervous,
and knowing nothing of the luxuries of our
modern civilization which do so much to en-
feeble the system and give us hot and tyran-
nous nerves. In his nineteenth year Chalmers
was licensed as a preacher by the Presbytery of
St. Andrew's. There is something almost piti-
able and ridiculous about boy preachers knowing so very little of life and its perplexities,
temptations and cares — knowing necessarily
so little of any lore except schoolboy lore, and
yet set to instruct matured or even aged Chris-

tian people in the things of the kingdom of God. One wonders less at their audacity than at the folly of the men who license them as preachers. Of course Chalmers at nineteen might be mentally as percipient as ordinary men at thirty. Preachers, like poets, are born, not made, and the slumbering possibilities in the youth may have been detected by those wise men of the St. Andrew's Presbytery.

He did not do much preaching for two years after receiving his license, but spent the winters in Edinburgh attending the lectures of the ablest professors at that University. In his twenty-fourth year he was ordained minister of Kilmany, a small parish in Fifeshire, about nine miles from St. Andrew's. He added to his ministerial work courses of lectures on chemistry in St. Andrew's, illustrated by experiments. These lectures were very popular. His studies seem to have been very varied — in chemistry, in mathematics, in political economy, of which he was very fond, a study which he pursued so thoroughly that in 1808, before he was thirty years of age, he had published a book entitled "An Inquiry into the Extent and Stability of National Resources."

At thirty years of age severe domestic bereavements, and a serious illness, which brought him near to death, laid him aside from all work for a year. During that year his mind underwent a great change. Up to that period his preaching had been more of the nature of exhortation to correct morals. From that time onward the higher elements of truth as set forth in the Gospels, in the teachings of Christ and his Apostles, were conspicuous in all his discourses. It was heart preaching thenceforth, not simply head preaching. He rose from his sick-bed a man consecrated to his work as never before. His whole soul seemed to be in everything he did. "He had seen the King in his beauty, and the land which is afar off." Henceforth the genius of his nature and his magnificent powers were devoted without reserve to the service of God and man. In his thirty-fifth year he was called to be a minister to the Tron Church and parish in Glasgow; called only by a narrow majority, for they did not like his exceeding Biblicalism.   In the midst of the crowded population of Glasgow the man developed into that largeness of which he was capable.   There was room for his greatness to show itself. His "Astronomical Discourses" — perhaps the most eloquent productions which ever fell from his pen or were poured out from his lips — thrust his fame up to a quite unparalleled height.   They were published after being preached.   Within a year nine editions and twenty thousand copies of the volume were in circulation.   They carried his fame to the metropolis of England, and on his appearance in London in the following year he was greeted by enthusiastic crowds.   From that time onward his fame remained.   And it has continued.   Scotland ranks no pulpit orator on a higher plane than he, judging from the marvelous influence which he had over every audience that came under the spell of his magnetic power.   Moreover, there was no clap-trap, no trickery, no aiming at effects, in his

methods. Everything produced in the pulpit
was carefully prepared in the study — almost
every word written; but it was all his own, in
method, style, diction, mode of utterance, and
effect of utterance. The preparation was an
exact laying down of the lines on which a great
locomotive, with fierce coals all aglow at the
heart of it, rushed to its destination, carrying
with it freight, passengers, and all at a rate at
which it would have been entirely impossible
for them to travel by themselves. As one has
put it, while Chalmers was preaching "there
was no possibility of sailing up his stream.
You must go with him, or you must go ashore."
"He was full of his idea, possessed by it,
moved altogether by its power; believing, he
spoke, and without stint or fear, often apparently contradicting his former self — careless
about everything, but speaking fully his mind."
His mind was so large, so capacious, there was
room in it for so much, everything around
him seemed anxious to contribute something
to the stores within; mathematics, poetry,
philosophy, political economy — they stood

round with imploring looks saying to him,
Take me and use me, and in your employ I
shall feel at my best, and be connected with
the God who made me ; thus enriched, ennobled
and glorified.

To criticise preachers is a thankless business, and specially as everybody assumes it
to be a business for which each has special
aptitude. But when we have before us a man
of Chalmers's greatness and competency, we
are tempted to say a word or two, in spite of
the seeming immodesty of its being done by
one who occupies a humble place among the
crowd. Chalmers died when I was a very
small boy, and so I cannot speak of him from
sight or hearing. But I have spoken with
men who heard him. From their accounts,
and from all that has been written about his
method and its results, it would seem that he
had much to overcome before he could get
himself fairly on the way. His accent was
Scottish, and very provincial at that. At first
there was no promise of what was coming.
He stumbled into what he had to say until

some great thought lit the fire within, and then began the flowing and raging of the stream, carrying all before it. Some preachers can preach to the cultured few, some to the thinking and inquiring middle classes of society, some can command the ear of the populace or a section of it; but it must be evident that he is the greatest as a preacher who can command all classes and conditions of men, for it must be clear that he appeals to the humanity in them and not to any surface differences. Moreover, the history of men of the pulpit shows that sectional men never are, nor ever can be, great preachers. It is the humanity in a man which makes him capable of that temperament without which you have the elegant essayist, or the literary critic, or the fastidious scholar, but not the real and true preacher. The real and true heart that was in Chalmers was shown after he had been at the Tron Church four years, when he expressed his earnest wish to be transferred to St. John's Church — a parish the population of which was made up princi-

pally of weavers, laborers, factory-workers
and other operatives. To this church he was
transferred, and the artisans of that district
had as their preacher the mightiest orator in
all Scotland, if not in Great Britain. Here
he wrought prodigiously to bring the two
thousand families in this crowded district under the influence of the Gospel. He divided
this great parish into twenty-five districts,
with a deacon and elder for each district —
the deacon to attend to the secularities, the
elder to the spiritualities. At the commence-
ment of his taking charge of this parish it
cost for the sustenance of the indigent poor
an amount equal to about seven thousand
dollars a year; at the end of four years the
pauper expenditure was about one thousand
and six hundred dollars a year. The idle, the
drunken, the worthless, he summarily rejected
after giving them a fair trial, and confined
himself to encouraging and helping those who
could, by a little wise help, be put on their
feet and made respectable members of society.
He soon found out that there were persons to

whom money help was only demoralization. So long as others would help them they would not help themselves. They became chronic paupers, caring nothing for sympathy and advice and encouragement, caring only for such loaves and fishes as came to them by the labor of some one else. These Chalmers left the civil authorities to care for as best they could, and reserved the church help and the visits of church helpers for people who manifestly had souls as well as mouths. But four years of such untiring labor as that he gave to this St. John's Parish broke him down in health, and he had to quit it, with a great load of experience which he has put into several volumes on the "Christian and Civic Economy of Large Towns," but with little strength left. Dr. Chalmers is an illustration of the fact that no man, though he have the strength of Hercules and the eloquence of Demosthenes, can dribble out his mental and sympathetic strength drop by drop, drop by drop, every day of the week, and have a river full of it to pour over and into an exacting audience on Sunday.

Dr. Chalmers had a whole army of assistants, and yet in four years he had to retire from this great and successful effort of his. When, at a meeting of students and ministers in London, the late Henry Ward Beecher was asked as to the possibility and utility of house-to-house visitation, he replied: "A man has only just so much vitality in his brain. If he spends it drop by drop all through the week, he cannot have it in any concentrated form on Sunday. There are communities where the average of knowledge is so low that the man as a pastor must sacrifice himself as a preacher, and must go round from house to house; but you cannot, in one case in ten thousand, unite the two." I am sure Mr. Beecher is right.

Any man preaching out of an exhausted vitality can never do much good to the intellects and hearts of his people. If we had a Scriptural ecclesiasticism, every man would find the work for which he is suited. The New Testament idea is one church in one town, with a varied ministry — of course more meeting-houses than one or two or three where the town was large. But nowadays we have to get on without being Scriptural, so far as our ecclesiasticisms are concerned. In 1823 Dr. Chalmers had to accept a Professorship of Moral Philosophy in the University of St. Andrew's. In five years more he was transferred to the Chair of Theology in the University of Edinburgh. As a Professor of Moral Philosophy he had especially insisted on this cardinal doctrine, "that a right moral condition is essential to a right economic condition of the masses;" that character is the parent of comfort, and that consequently you can never get irreligious communities right by any readjustment of economic and social relations. It is the old principle, "Make the tree good, and the fruit will be good."

That is where people who write on political economy and on socialism are ever making a mistake. Given ten thousand bad men, how to so arrange them that the total will be good? It is a hopeless problem so long as it stands so. During his professorships Dr. Chalmers was continually using his pen, and continually preaching as Sundays brought him opportunity. Soon a crisis came in the history of his church, in which a leader of men was necessary. The civil and ecclesiastical courts came into collision. Incapable men were appointed to churches against the protest of congregations. The evil became unendurable. Finally, with Dr. Chalmers as their leader, on the eighteenth of May, 1843, four hundred and seventy clergymen withdrew from the general assembly and founded the Free Church of Scotland. The first moderator was Chalmers himself. The remaining years of his life were given to building up the Free Church and in perfecting his great work, "Institutes of Theology." These years were few. This great secession, the last great church movement in which conscience has been magnificently supreme over considerations of a pecuniary and social sort, took place in 1843.

In 1847, Chalmers passed away, so peacefully that none were witnesses of his departure. On Sabbath evening, May 30, he bade his family good-night. Next morning, when his room was entered and the curtains of his bed withdrawn, he was found half-erect, his head leaning gently back upon the pillow, no token of pain or struggle, the brow and hand, when touched, so cold as to indicate that some hours had already elapsed since the spirit had peacefully departed.

Whether it be correct or not to call Dr. Chalmers an original thinker, it is certainly correct to affirm that the old thought became new in its interest and force when he passed it through the fervid alembic of his own mind. It has been well said that an old truth immediately becomes new when you put it into practice. The Christian religion immediately became a new power and force for the resistance of evil and the promotion of good when it found incarnation in the personality of Dr. Chalmers ; his book on the " Adaptation of External Nature to the Moral and Intellectual Constitution of Man " is a great work, had great influence, and shows great thinking power.

The power of his personality was great because he was so simple and childlike in his
nature. Like so many other men of first-rate
genius, his childhood seems to have been pre-
served and carried up into his manhood. He
realized that which Coleridge says is the true
condition of unsophisticated life — " Every
man should include all his former selves in
the present, as a tree has its former years'
growths inside its last;" so Dr. Chalmers bore
along with him his childhood, his youth, his
early and full manhood into his mature old
age — if he can correctly be said to have at-
tained to a mature old age at all. One who
knew him well writes of him : " In simplicity
he was a child. By simplicity we do not
mean the simplicity of the head — of that he
had none — but we refer to a certain quality
of heart and of life which gives a directness
to all actions and a certain beautiful unconsciousness of self — an outgoing of the whole
nature that we see in children. D'Alembert
speaks of it in Fénelon as a characteristic of
him. It is a quality which renders the pos-

sessor dear to others. Sincerity may be hard,
harsh and unlovable. Simplicity is more than
sincerity. It affects neither virtue nor truth.
It is never occupied with itself. It seems to
have lost this Ego of which one is so jealous."
Chalmers had no idea of looking after his "re-
spectability" and "dignity"; of keeping his
status or maintaining his position. They who
are thus occupied are invariably too self-conscious ever to be for long either amiable or
useful. Self-consciousness kills everything.
No man or woman can do a thing well so long
as they are conscious of themselves as of any
very great dignity or importance, or so long as
they are conscious of doing the thing. To set
one part of yourself to stand off and watch
the other part of yourself is fatal to all effi-
ciency. Gough used to say that he never could
speak freely until he had lost all thought of
himself and how he was doing a thing, and
felt only the theme and the audience. I apprehend that is so with all effective speakers.

This writer from whom I have quoted as
personally well knowing Dr. Chalmers says:

" He was, like Agamemnon, a native leader of
men, and, with all his homeliness of feature
and deportment, and his perfect simplicity of
expression, there was about him that divinity
that doth hedge a king." You felt a power in
him and going forth from him, drawing you to
him in spite of yourself. There is to us a con-
tinual mystery in this power of one man over
another. We find it acting everywhere with
the simplicity, the ceaselessness, the energy
of gravitation; it is proportioned to bulk, for
we hold to the notion of a bigness in souls as
well as in bodies — one soul differing from another in quantity and momentum as well as in
quality and force. Jonathan Edwards speaks
of a man of spiritual influence as having more
being than another.

Dr. Chalmers's question often was, when
asking about a man — " Is he a man of
wecht ? " By " wecht " he meant force,
energy, the suggestion of power.

Generally such men as those to whom Dr.
Chalmers referred in this word are men of
capacious understanding, strong will; an emo-

tional nature, quick, powerful, urgent, undeni-
able, in perpetual communication with the
energetic will, and the large, resolute intellect;
and a strong, hearty, capable body — the mind
finding its way at once and in full to the face,
to the gesture, to every act of the body.

And yet these endowments must never be
held in statuesque stiffness, or they will immediately become feeble. In Dr. Chalmers's
days and in his country they knew little, if
anything, of vocal culture or of any kind of
elocutionary training. The thing is good in
itself as tending to give a man possession of
himself, and to correct faults. But if it becomes a harness on a man, in which he cannot
move, except with a limited degree of freedom,
or if it should become what is very much worse,
a strait-jacket (corset, I believe, is the politer
word), pressing in the ribs and creating de-
formity, then I should say, away with it!
The fastidious people of the world would not
have endured Chalmers's provincialisms, but
when the torrent of his mental power rushed
down upon them, and submerged their self-

consciousness, they might then have felt that
he had "wecht," and that there was something
divine in the man.

Have you never observed how some people
pass through life as if "all the world were a
stage, and all the men and women merely
players "? Every step of the way and every
hour of the day they suggest the actor. And
children, poor little mortals! are taught to be
actors — that is the worst of all the miseries
of this wretchedly artificial life of ours. I
think that our nineteenth century civilization
never looks so hideous as when it has produced a fashionable child — a little mortal with
all the politenesses engrafted on its tongue,
and all its sweet natural spontaneousness and
simplicity gone. There is all the difference in
the world between allowing children to be
cruel and selfish and rude, and allowing them
to be sweet and spontaneous and childlike.

Does it not indicate how simple and childlike Chalmers was — the fact we are told of
him that when, one Saturday, he was at a
friend's house near the Pentlands, he collected

all the children and small people — the other
bairns as he called them — and with no one else
of his own growth took the lead to the nearest
hill-top; how he made each take the biggest
and roundest stone he could find and carry;
how he panted up the hill himself with one of
enormous size; how he kept up their hearts
and made them shout with glee, with the light
of his countenance, and with all his pleasant
and strange ways and words; how, having got
the little breathless men and women to the
top of the hill, he, hot and scant of breath,
looked round upon the world and upon them
with his broad, benignant smile; how he set
off his own huge "fellow"; how he watched
him setting out on his race, slowly, stupidly,
vaguely at first, almost as if he might die before he began to live, then suddenly giving a
spring and off like a shot, bounding, tearing,
acquiring strength in going; how he spoke to,
upbraided him, cheered him, gloried in him,
all but prayed for him; how he joked philosophy to his wondering and ecstatic crew
when he (the stone) disappeared among some

brackens, telling them that they had the evidence of their senses that he was in, they might even know he was there by his effects, by the moving brackens, himself unseen ; how plain it became that he had gone in, when he actually came out; how he ran up the opposite side a bit, and then fell back and lazily expired at the bottom; how, to the astonishment of these little folk, he took from each his cherished stone and set it off himself, showing them how they all ran alike, yet differently ; how he went on " making," as he said, " an induction of particulars " till he came to the Benjamin of the flock, a wee, wee man, who had brought up a stone bigger than his own big head; then how he let him set off his own ; and how wonderfully it ran — what miraculous leaps ! what escapes from impossible places ! and how it ran up the other side further than any, and, by some felicity, remained there ? (See Dr. John Brown.)

Who can read all this and not love Chalmers ? Here we see the child carried up into and held in solution in the man ; here, too, we get a glimpse into the secret of his greatness—viz., his sympathy with all life everywhere around him, with the life of children as with the life of the great striving multitudes of people in the crowded district of St. John's, Glasgow. In this we find him to be one with other great men his contemporaries in Great Britain. Indeed, it seems to be a sign of greatness, this practical sympathy with struggling humanity; more than anything else does it betoken Christliness of spirit and largeness of soul. When I recall the names of other Scottish Presbyterians of modern days — men translated to the majority — Norman McLeod and Thomas Guthrie — the same intense interest in the classes in society who are put at a disadvantage shows itself. When, crossing the border, I think of other men who now no longer walk the streets of this Vanity Fair — Frederick Robertson, Charles Kingsley, Frederick Denison Maurice — it is the same with them as with Chalmers. The question how can I help my fellow-men who are struggling and poor — this was an inquiry in which they never ceased to be interested. Dr. Hanna, the son-in-law of Chalmers, the compiler of that most interesting biography in which we get nearer to the heart of the great man than elsewhere, says of him: "The dearest object of his earthly existence was the elevation of the common people."

Chalmers had studied political economy with a thoroughness possible to only few, and came from the study more than ever a believer in the disappointment and failure which must attend all social reforms that do not treat man as man ; namely, as body and soul. Men must be elevated morally and intellectually if they are to be elevated socially. It is this great radical fact which is too generally ignored by labor reformers and all socialists who are not Christian socialists. When Chalmers, with an insight which came of Christian perception, opened a Sunday-school in almost every street in his great, but poor district in Glasgow, so that the school should be in sight of the homes of all the people, he did more in a few years to raise the moral tone of the district than could be done in a century apart from this appeal to the heart and mind of the people. I believe in every family having a home — a house, however small, complete in itself — in which they have independence and privacy. There is more moral influence in this than people think. Flats, lodging-houses, tenement-houses, *et hoc genus omne,* may be temporary necessities, but as permanent places of residence they are one and all demoralizing. There is too much Arabism in the world. We do not want to increase the number of the Arab class. Religion and morals have always been associated with, and always will be associated with home life. I venture the prediction that if ever we should have great social upheavals in the cities of this country, such as will shake society to its foundations, the city which of all others will suffer the least will be Philadelphia, because there are twice as many people who own their houses as in any other large city. I am further persuaded that ministers of the Gospel must take hold of these social questions to elevate them before

ever there will be any peaceful solution of the
economic difficulties which threaten us as well
as other nations. It is only once and again
that a Dr. Chalmers rises into view, with great
human sympathies joined to transcendent abili-
ties; but no one, or ten, or a hundred men,
however plentifully endowed they might be,
can do more than put a finger to the great
work which God calls all Christian men to
help to do. The writer in the " Encyclopædia
Britannica " says of Chalmers: " Various elements combined to clothe him with public
influence — a childlike, guileless, transparent
simplicity, the utter absence of anything
factitious in matter or manner, a kindliness of
nature that made him flexible to every human
sympathy, a chivalry of sentiment that raised
him above all the petty jealousies of public
life, a firmness of purpose that made vacilla-
tion almost a thing impossible, a force of will
and general momentum that bore all that was
movable before it, a vehement utterance and
overwhelming eloquence that gave him command of the multitude, a scientific reputation

that won for him the respect and attention of
the more educated, the legislative faculty that
framed measures upon the broadest principles,
the practical sagacity that adapted them to
the ends they were intended to realize, a
purity of motive that put him above all suspicion of selfishness, and a piety unobtrusive,
but most profound, simple, yet ardent."

Such a testimony indicates to us how varied
and great were his gifts, and how thoroughly
he consecrated them to the highest uses known
on earth to man. The sense of greatness impressed everybody — great in his conceptions,
great in his sweep of thought, great in his
plans, great in his zeal — yet with it the beautiful unconsciousness that he was great. There
are to be found quite a number of prompt, zealous, earnest men up and down in our churches,
but, as one has said, they are so unforgettingly
self-conscious, " apt to run wild, to get need-
lessly brisk, unpleasantly incessant. A weasel
is good or bad as the case may be — good
against vermin, bad to meddle with ; but inspired weasels, weasels on a mission, are ter-

rible indeed, mischievous and fell — 'fierce as wild bulls, untamable as flies.'" Chalmers did not like these men — they had not *wecht*, as he said. Weight was an essential thing with him. "When the sun sets," writes Dr. John Brown, in speaking of Chalmers, "he rises elsewhere — he goes on rejoicing like a strong man running his race. So does a great man; when he leaves us and our concerns he rises elsewhere; and we may reasonably suppose that one who has in this world played a great part in its greatest histories, who has through a long life been pre-eminent for promoting the good of men and the glory of God, will be looked upon with keen interest when he joins the company of the immortals. They must have heard of his fame, they may, in their ways, have seen and helped him already."

This we have on authority. "They that be teachers shall shine as the brightness of the firmament, and they that have turned many to righteousness as the stars for ever and ever."

V.

FREDERICK W. ROBERTSON.

IN modern days no man of the pulpit has excited more interest than the Rev. F. W. Robertson. There is something phenomenal about him. While he lived his brief life, his influence was confined to a fashionable watering place forty miles from London. Since his death he has preached to tens of thousands. Wherever the English language is spoken, and beyond, Robertson's Sermons have been read and re-read. "Except a corn of wheat fall into the ground and die, it abideth alone; but if it die, it bringeth forth much fruit." That passage has been quoted over and over as expressing the method through which Robertson has gained his

unique influence. Those of you who have
read his biography and those wonderful letters
with which it is crowded, know far more about
him than I can even suggest. I am not about
to criticise his sermons; that in me would be
an impertinence. Nor am I about to recall
the recorded events in his life — a life all too
brief, yet long enough for the highest order of
usefulness. It is hardly possible to move
along a line of remark which has not already
been traveled by others with more knowledge,
and therefore with firmer tread than to me is
possible. But the more I think of Robertson
the more unique does he become.

The eldest of seven children, he was born
February 3, 1816, in London. His grandfather a colonel in the British army, his father
a captain in the Royal Artillery, Frederick
Robertson inherited a soldier's temperament,
and was always complaining that his life had
been turned out of its natural course. When
nearly at the end of his career, he writes:
" As I walked home in my dragoon cloak, I
thought I ought to be at this moment lying in

it at rest at Moodkee, where the Third fought
so gallantly, and where spots of brighter
green than usual are the only record to mark
where the flesh of heroes is melting into its
kindred dust again." The many removals
from place to place of his family while a child
— the first five years of his life in Fort Leith,
then at Beverley in Yorkshire, then at Tours,
then back again to England — such a roving
existence is generally very unfavorable to a
pious training of youth; but Robertson seems
to have been very carefully trained, until at
sixteen he was placed in the New Academy,
Edinburgh.

As a boy he had the intensity and sensitiveness which characterized his manhood. Everything beautiful appealed to him. He was passionately fond of nature, passionately fond of
animals and birds; in character, chivalrous
and imaginative; he had, too, a clear sense
of duty, and was devout and reverent withal.
Prayer seems to have been natural to him
from the earliest dawn of intelligence. To all
pure souls, most likely, it is natural, but the

boy Robertson felt it was good for all occasions, and not merely for religious occasions.

"I remember, when a very young boy," he writes, "going out shooting with my father, and praying, as often as the dogs came to a point, that he might kill the bird. As he did not always do this, and as sometimes there would occur false points, my heart got bewildered. I believe I began to doubt some times the efficacy of prayer, sometimes the lawfulness of field sports. Once, too, I recollect, when I was taken up with nine other boys at school to be unjustly punished, I prayed to escape the shame. The master, previously to flogging all the others, said to me, to the great bewilderment of the whole school, 'Little boy, I excuse you; I have particular reasons for it.' And, in fact, I was never flogged during the three years I was at that school. That incident settled my mind for a long time; only I doubt whether it did me any good, for prayer became a charm. I fancied myself the favorite of the Invisible. I knew that I carried about a talisman which would save me from all harm. It did not make me better; it simply gave me security, as the Jew felt safe in being the descendant of Abraham, or went into battle under the protection of the ark, sinning no less all the time."

For a little time after leaving this school, Robertson was in a lawyer's office; this he utterly detested and abominated; he longed to go into the army. When his father, who knew the young man better than he knew himself, suggested to him to go to college and prepare for the Christian ministry, his reply was decided — " Anything but that; I am not fit for it."

It seemed for a time as if the army was his destiny. His name was put down on the list for a cavalry regiment serving in India. Before his departure he made the acquaintance, casually, as it seemed, of a Mr. Davis, and his course from that hour seemed to be changed. The change came about in a very singular way — in fact, it came about from the barking of a dog. Lady Trench resided next door to Captain Robertson; she had a daughter seriously ill; the young lady was prevented from sleeping by the barking of Captain Robertson's dog. The families were strangers to each other, but Lady Trench wrote to beg that the dog might be removed; the dog was not only removed, but in so kind and acquiescent a manner that Lady Trench called to express her thanks. She was so much struck with the bearing of the eldest son that an intimacy sprang up between the families which resulted in the introduction of young Robertson to some of Lady Trench's clerical friends, and they insisted that he should look in another direction than the army for his life work. The result was he soon went to the University of Oxford to begin mental preparation. Referring afterward to the singular change that came in his course of life, he writes. "All is free," he says — "that is false; all is fated — that is false. All things are free and fated — that is true. I cannot overthrow the argument of the man who says that everything is fated, or, in other words, that God orders all things, and cannot change that order. If I had not met a certain person, I should not have changed my profession; if I had not known a certain lady, I should not probably have met this person; if that lady had not had a delicate daughter who was disturbed by the barking of my dog, if my dog had not barked that night, I should now have been in the dragoons, or fertilizing the soil of India. Who can say that these things were not ordered, and that apparently the merest trifles did not produce failure and a marred existence?" To the barking of a dog we probably owe those volumes of sermons, which have, perhaps, influenced more thoughtful minds than any other sermons preached in the nineteenth century.

Well, Robertson was at Oxford at the time when Newman was in the flood tide of his influence. He must have heard Newman again and again. What special influence he had over such a sensitive and receptive mind we cannot tell, but Robertson's mind was too discriminating to be swept into any stream and carried down with the current. While at Oxford two greater men than Newman seemed to have

produced an influence over him for good.   A
brilliant course of lectures on history was
given by Dr. Arnold (of Rugby).   All that
was most wise and most distinguished thronged
the University Theater in order to listen to
him.   On another occasion there appeared one
whose poetry had influenced Robertson's mind
more powerfully than the poetry of almost
any other.   We feel the influence of Wordsworth over Robertson.   It forces itself into
recognition in his sermons, and especially in
his letters.   We must not linger over these
formative influences, as it is to Robertson as a
preacher rather than as a thinker our attention
is drawn.   He left Oxford, received ordina-
tion, began his ministry, first in Winchester,
then in Cheltenham — in both positions as an
assistant — then for a very brief period at
Oxford, and finally at Brighton, with which
town his name is forever associated.   He began
his ministry as one attached to the evangelical
party in the church.   He ended it at Brighton,
at the early age of thirty-seven years, virtually
cast out by all parties.

When I think of his departure hence at that
age, and of the influence he has exerted —
when also it is taken into account that that
influence belongs mainly to the last seven
years of his life — it is almost incredible that
any human being could crowd so much thinking into so brief a space of time. I believe
that no one can do it and live. Robertson
himself seems to me an illustration of the fact.
He was a man of naturally robust constitution,
but the fires within were so hot that they
burnt up the house in which they were lit.
He was so sensitive to all influences in nature
and in social life that his joy, when he had it,
was too great for mortal man, and his suffering when it came was too intense to be sup-
portable. Undoubtedly he was a martyr to
his own nobility. His very greatness and
goodness made him capable of a degree of
mental suffering in presence of evil of which
ordinary men have not the faintest conception.
Any man who is blessed (or cursed — which-
ever word we may employ) with an ideal so
lofty as that of Robertson's must of necessity

have a sad life and a sad ministry, as Cæsar
Malan predicted of Robertson. Any man who
is intensely individual, who thinks more deeply
and with more thoroughness than his fellow-
men, must expect to find misunderstanding
and suspicion dogging his steps. Just as that
portion of the female world which calls itself
"society" never forgives a woman for dressing
out of the fashion, so that portion of the religious world which represents the Pharisees
of the olden time never forgives a man for
thinking ahead of the fashion of his day. The
church to which Robertson belonged had in it
then, and has now, three parties, or schools —
High, Low, and Broad. In Robertson's young
manhood Arnold stood for the Broad Church,
Newman for the High Church, men like Close
of Cheltenham, Stowell of Manchester, and
McNeile of Liverpool, for the Low Church.
The Evangelical school was then in the ascend-
ency in the Episcopal Church of England. It
is so no longer. The reason of it is that it
became too sectarian, too mechanical in its interpretation of Scripture, and too inconsistent

with itself, to maintain its influence. It ceased
to grow, and when anything ceases to grow it
ceases to live.

Great men like Robertson have to do their
own thinking, and the men who help them
to think are sure to become their friends.
Wordsworth had helped Robertson to see God
in nature, Arnold had helped him to see God in
history, and his own continuous study of the
Bible and of the best literature of his own
day had helped him to see God in humanity.
And so all things in nature, and all men of
eminence in letters, seemed to come to his
open, truthful, discriminating nature with some
tribute, and he grew out of all parties. "God
and the human soul" he came to know — nothing else. How could the High Churchmen
feel kindly toward a man who wrote : "I can
not say how much it has impressed me with
the feeling that these apparently innocent
things — Apostolic Succession and High Views
(as they are called) of the Christian Sacraments
— are really anti-Christian in their operation.
When they take shape in actual life, they

reveal their meaning to be a doctrine of election, which is just so much worse than the common one that it is external and official, and which, moreover, renders the sacraments themselves uncertain in their efficacy by demanding the co-operation of the will of the minister if the reception of them is to be savingly beneficial. How destructive the doctrine must be of all simple and immediate fellowship between man and man and between man and God I need not say."

How could the men who thought that to save " Standards of Doctrine " was everything be on the most amiable terms with a man who could write: " There is no substitute for the light within us revealing the light of God. Standards of doctrine do often more harm than good; and by their very definitions and externalities lead the mind away from God instead of to him." Yet we must not suppose that the word " liberal," as we use it here in New England, was applicable to Robertson. That which he saw to be truth he held with a tenaciousness, and bowed down to it with

a reverence which indicated that his heart was
wholly and entirely in it. No worship could
be more passionate, more profound, than his
worship of God's Christ. But he saw that
man's conception of truth can never measure
the truth as it is in the mind of God; that as
the mind of a man becomes purer and freer, so
his conception of the truth as it is in Jesus
must become larger and grander. "God's
truth," he says, "must be boundless. Tracta-
rians and Evangelicals suppose that it is a
pond which you can walk round and say, 'I
hold the truth.' What! all? Yes, all! There
it is, circumscribed, defined, proved, quite large
enough to be the immeasurable Gospel of the
Lord of the Universe!" What about creeds?
we ask him. They are useful, he replies, as
aids to faith, but intolerable as limitations of
faith. It is customary to say that Robertson
lived before his time; that if he had lived in
our generation he would have received better
treatment from the ecclesiastics of our day
than he received from the ecclesiastics of that
English State Church to which he belonged

only in name. I am not so sure of that. Robertson died in 1853. He is one of the most modern of thinkers in the Church of our day.

It is true that an immense change has come over the religious life of England since the death of this great thinker. It would be very difficult to get up any persecution in England now against any clergyman who showed himself as true to the Christ of God and to the Scripture as did Robertson. And this recognition of a man's right to go to the Scriptures for himself and receive the instruction of apostles and prophets at first hand is largely attributable to the seed sown by this eminent man of whom we are thinking. Now, we must always try to cherish a charitable spirit even toward those who persecute others. I know how exceedingly difficult it is to credit the persecutor with anything good. To a man whose spirit has been bathed again and again in the bath of regeneration which Scripture truth affords, the conduct of the Vicar of Brighton toward a man like Robertson does seem atrocious. To us

standing afar off and looking at both it rouses
within us hot indignation to find a hard official
like him of Brighton hindering the over-
wrought Robertson from obtaining the assistant whose help might have saved Robertson
for a few more years of useful life. But it is
in the nature of things that such a man as that
Vicar of Brighton could not understand or
sympathize with a man of such a high order of
genius as the minister of Trinity Chapel.
While in a very real sense Robertson's intensity and zeal killed him, yet is it also true that
in his last days he was sacrificed to the want
of sympathy which arose out of the low order
of intellect and corresponding narrow affec-
tional nature of those around him. The Vicar
of Brighton was his ecclesiastical superior,
and to have in his neighborhood such a man
as this, whose sympathies were with the poor-
est as ardently as with others in society, to
whom workingmen looked with a reverence
that was new to them, for whom servant girls
had an affection as if he were their elder
brother, to whom soldiers went as recognizing

in him the true type of the Red Cross knight,
to hear whom lawyers took a journey on Saturday from London and remained till Monday at
Brighton, that High Church machinist — ecclesiastic I mean — could not understand it; how
could he? John the Baptist in the neighborhood of Herod was not a more unwelcome
voice.

There is always something blind and cruel
about the religious persecutor. He is blind,
for he persuades himself that he is doing God
service, when he is really serving Antichrist.
He is blind, for he seldom understands, or puts
himself to the trouble to understand, the man
whom he persecutes. He assumes that he (the
persecutor) is right, and cannot but be right.
There is very little room for doubt that when
the Pharisees and Sadducees crucified Jesus of
Nazareth they persuaded themselves that it
was done to preserve the nation and the true
religion. Many, if not most of these men
were sincere, but they were wrong all the
same. The cruelest men in the world are the
men who are sincere and wrong at the same

time.　The men who put Jesus to death were
the destroyers of their nation; he would have
been its saviour.　Zeal without knowledge is
the fire that burns the house down, not the fire
that warms the atmosphere into a summer
temperature.　Not zeal alone, or sincerity
alone, but a total submission to the mind and
will of Christ, heart-sympathy with him and
his redeeming work for man, a sympathy
which will not allow us to be hard or cruel —
that is the Christian spirit.　We often talk of
zeal for truth, and try to justify conduct that
does not look Christian in spirit and temper
by this plea, that the truth must be maintained
at all hazards.　But what is truth?　"I am
the truth," says Jesus the Christ.　We may
take his words of love and make paving-stones
of them to throw at heretics.　We may be as
zealous as the disciples who wanted to call
down fire from heaven on those who were not
of their way of thinking; but Jesus rebuked
them, and said, "Ye know not what spirit ye
are of."　In the light of Scripture there was
no justification for the cruel and heartless con-

duct of that Vicar of Brighton who let poor
Robertson die rather than allow him to have
the man he wanted as a helper in the work at
Trinity Chapel. The greatest thinker, one
only excepted, who has appeared in the English pulpit in our century was sacrificed to
heartless officialism. "If the highest work of
thought," says one, " is to illuminate a subject,
to pierce to its heart and unfold in creative
order all its parts, and not merely to tell you
about it and what others have thought about
it — to make alive a new order of ideas, and
not merely to explain an old order — then
Frederick Robertson takes rank as among
the great thinkers of modern times." "He
not only went into a subject and around it,
but he pictured it. He made it alive; he
pierced it through and through with light
and life."

Of course the attitudinarians and the platitu-
dinarians called this man dangerous, even social-
istic. He believed that workingmen had as
real a property in Christianity as had other
men — that it specially belonged to them; and

sought to bring Christianity into the workshop, and into the common business of life. That was called Socialism. Some of you may remember that passage which occurs in an address given to workingmen about infidel publications in the Town Hall of Brighton. It evidenced that Christ was to him the overpowering manifestation of the Divine Presence — that the most innate, most sacred love in his nature was his love to God's Christ:

" I refuse to permit discussion respecting the love which a Christian man bears his Redeemer — a love more delicate far than the love which was ever borne to sister or the adoration with which he regards his God — a reverence more sacred than ever man bore to mother."

Christ and the soul — these were his constant study. To attempt to show in what respects his treatment of the doctrines of the Christian religion was peculiar would occupy too much space for our present limitations.

As to his personal character, there was in it a dignity which seemed so natural to him that

it offended none, a chivalry which made him
daring and noble, a purity which seemed stain-
less. He was undoubtedly fastidious, and in
him there was that morbid streak which one
finds so generally in the most sensitive and
greatest minds. Nothing could offend him more
than to call him " a popular preacher." He
knew by what base arts popularity was often
won, and he despised it. The terrible reaction
that came after such intense preaching made
him almost despise popular address. The
vanity and fastidiousness of a fashionable
watering-place rasped him all the time. Take
such an extract as this : " I wish I did not
hate preaching so much; the degradation of
being a Brighton preacher is almost intolerable. ' I cannot dig — to beg I am ashamed,'
but I think there is not a hard-working artisan
who does not seem to me a worthier and a
higher being than myself. How humiliated
and degraded to the dust I have felt in per-
ceiving myself quietly taken for the popular
preacher of a fashionable watering-place ; how
slight the power seems to me to be given by it

of winning souls ; and how sternly I have kept
my tongue from saying a syllable or a sentence
in pulpit or on platform because it would be
popular ! "

This is morbid, possibly, and yet I have an
idea that many other preachers than Robertson
know something of a similar state of mind in
those times of reaction which follow the most
intense efforts of speech.

Whatever his critics may have had to say
of an adverse and captious quality about
Robertson, who does not feel in heart-sympathy with him when we find such a passage
as this :

" When we gaze on the perfect righteousness
of Christ, and are able to say, There, that is
my religion, that is what I want to be, that is
what I am not, that is my offering, that is my
life as I would wish to give it — my Saviour,
fill up the blurred and blotted sketch which
my clumsy hand has drawn of a divine life
with the fullness of thy perfect picture ! — I
feel the beauty which I cannot realize. Robe
me in thine unutterable purity.

" 'Rock of ages, cleft for me,
  Let me hide myself in thee.' "

These brief and most fragmentary remarks
are not to be taken as anything more than
mere notes on Robertson and his influence.
Thinking men and thinking women will relish
Robertson, but spiritual consumptives and
Pharisees and Sadducees hardly at all. Yet
he remains a mighty power for generations yet
unborn. His sermons will be read and re-read
as long as Christian disciples are found. "As
I read his life," says one, " it seems to me we
are reading a story of Christian knighthood."

Before the valley of the shadow of death
was entered, he seemed to know that he must
die young, and so crowded into his life all the
work he could do. And when he entered the
valley the presence of God sustained him.
When scarcely able to move, a day or two before he died, he rose at four o'clock in the
morning and crept to the window to see as he
said, the " beautiful morning." The beauty of
the light and of the sun, and of the trees and
works of God in nature, always calmed him.

A night or two before his death he dreamed that his two sisters, long since dead, came to crown him. "I saw them," he said earnestly. All reverent kindnesses were heaped around his dying bed. "How different," he said, "the lot of Him who would fain have slaked his morning hunger with green figs." His dear and attached friend, Lady Byron, left a sick-bed to see him, but was permitted to be with him only a few moments. He suffered most acutely; the brain could hardly endure it; yet he never lost consciousness. When they would change his position he could not endure the touch, and said: "I cannot bear it; let me rest. I must die; let God do his work."

These were his last words; immediately afterward all was over. Fatal thirty-seven! the age of Byron, the age of Burns, the age of Raphael, and of many others whose sun never knew what it was to pass the noonday hour of this earthly life. For one day Brighton knew no sect and no party. Orthodox and heterodox, men of all religions and ecclesiastical schools, knew each other around Frederick

Robertson's grave only as men — sinning men, redeemed men. Jews, Unitarians, Roman Catholics, Quakers, all followed to the tomb this rarest and noblest of men. Lady Byron followed on foot. She would not go in her carriage, she said, after the remains of such a man. That silent voice was only then beginning to speak. It was as if God himself should say to that cruel ecclesiastic who had helped to kill him : " Now, for the first time, he enters his pulpit, and soon thronging thousands shall listen to his voice; wherever Christ is worshiped truly, there shall the voice of my servant speak." To how many men has he been a fountain of inspiration ! How many of us ministers have heard his words as if God spake to us through him : " This is the ministry and its work — not to drill hearts and minds and consciences into right forms of thought and mental postures, but to guide to the living God who speaks." " My brethren, if any man or any body of men stand between us and the living God, saying, 'Only through us, the church, can you approach God; only through my consecrated touch can you receive grace; only through my ordained teaching can you hear God's voice; and the voice which speaks in your soul, in the still moments of existence, is no revelation from God, but a delusion and a fanaticism' — that man is a false priest. To bring the soul face to face with God and supersede ourselves, that is the work of the Christian ministry." Principal Tulloch says: "Robertson has taught us 'that men will advance in religion as in everything else, not by displacement, but by expansion, by building the temple of truth to a loftier height. Few minds have enriched Christian thought more in our time, or given it a more healthy or sounder impulse."

VI.

EMANUEL SWEDENBORG.

THIS is one of the modern leaders of thought in whom there is no little of interest, and about whom we ought to know something. He is of several generations prior to any of those of whom we have spoken, but his influence as a theological teacher belongs specially to the last sixty or seventy years. To me, as to so many others, he is an enigma. His claims for himself as a revealer of the spiritual world are immense. Those claims have been allowed by a select number of people who have taken him as their religious teacher and guide, and have given to him an allegiance greater than that which we Biblicalists give to the Apostles — greater even than

the ordinary Christian gives to his Christ.
Those who would know the utmost that can be
said for the claims of Swedenborg to the allegiance which many minds give him should
read an English book called "Noble's Appeal"
—' a book, I must own, which, when I read it
twenty years ago, fascinated me not a little.

It is not in my purpose or plan in these brief
expositions of the leaders of thought in the
modern church to defend or accuse any who
give in their adhesion to them or dissent from
them. Believing that Christian congregations
ought to get all the instruction they will take,
and that it is much better to have intelligent
than unintelligent Christian people, my aim is
simply to give information, and in an uncon-
troversial way to express opinions whenever it
seems necessary. In days gone by I have read
enough of Swedenborg's writings to enable me
to say that I am acquainted with most of his
leading positions. It would not be honest or
fair for me to speak about him if I had only
such knowledge as people pick up from others
— such knowledge as floats into the mind on

the rippling current of conversation. Knowledge gained in that fashion is as fragmentary
and unreliable as knowledge can well be.
Even an honest and intelligent man's report of
another man's views and opinions is not often
to be trusted. The eminent ability that we
have of misunderstanding one another is to me
more and more remarkable. It is scarcely
ever safe or just to receive at second-hand the
opinions and teachings of any man of active
and independent research. Every mind seems
to possess its own coloring and refracting
medium. Without in the slightest degree in-
tending to be dishonest, men are dishonest.
Sweet reasonableness is as rare as soured prejudice is common. The poet has said that "an
honest man's the noblest work of God," but
that noblest work is seldom met with. I believe that it is easier for a miser to give one
hundred thousand dollars to charities than it
is for the most of men to be honest and fair
and just to all they meet. And so, if I want
to know what a great man teaches, I feel in
duty bound to go to his own books, not to

those of his commentators, be they friends or
enemies. On this principle I have read no
little of what would be called heresy in my
time, with the result to myself of making me
perceive that God has not put the whole of his
truth into any one man — except into the One
who came to be the Archetype of Humanity as
it is in the mind of God; with the result of
helping me to perceive how immensely superior
the New Testament is to anything and everything else in literature. If in my earliest
days I had not been taught that everything
is to be tested by the mind and spirit and
teaching and person of Jesus the Christ, I
should have suffered great damage and harm
from this unrestrained mental traveling. I am
convinced that it is not good for young people
to be allowed to wander here, there, and everywhere. Until the years of discretion have
arrived, it seems to me to have been designed
by God that fathers and mothers should exercise control over the moral, mental, and physical life of their children. The quality and
direction of a young person's life will, far

more than we seem to recognize, depend on the books they read and the company they keep. Liberty belongs to those who are of full growth, not to infants. Training and discipline belong to these. But I must not dwell within the area of these general remarks. A few facts as to the life of Emanuel Swedenborg before he reached the age of fifty-four, when the change came to him, or the stage in development when he claims that the spiritual world was opened to him.

He was born in Stockholm in 1688, and died in London in 1772. He lived eighty-four years on this planet. Thirty years of that eighty-four were consecrated to the study of theology and matters suggested or " revealed " (as he would say) to him about the spiritual world. Up to fifty-five years of age he was one of the most remarkable of scientific men. He was an assessor of mines ; a military engineer ; a great traveler — visiting England, Holland, France, and Germany when traveling was much more laborious work than it is now. His mind seems to have been intensely active; his in-

ventiveness great beyond almost any man of
his age ; he wrote on such subjects as decimal
money, on finding the longitude at sea by the
moon, on docks, sluices, and salt works, and on
very many other mathematical, scientific, and
practical themes.

To enumerate his scientific works is to cata-
logue a library. In some of them he antici-
pated recent discoveries. These are some of
his titles : " Principia ; or, The First Principles
of Natural Things ; being New Attempts toward a Philosophical Explanation of the Ele-
mentary World ; " " The Infinite and the Final
Cause of Creation, and the Intercourse between
the Soul and the Body ; " " The Animal Kingdom," one of his most delightful books. His
studies on the relation of matter to mind seem
to have been transitional to that subtler and
intenser theme which engrossed his attention
for the last thirty years of his life. In 1756
he published in London, in eight quarto Latin
volumes, his " Arcana Cælestia," a revelation
of the inner sense of Genesis and Exodus.
From this time onward he appears before the

world as a seer, as one whose interior sight is
opened to the order and the personalities of
the spiritual world. The many volumes of his
which are occupied with these themes, regard
them as we will — as visions similar to those
of Dante, or as visions dissimilar from those
of any other man — are to the last degree mys-
terious and wonderful. I do not undertake to
interpret or account for Swedenborg. No such
man has appeared in the history of these later
times. He is unique. To me he is a problem
I cannot solve — a profundity I cannot fathom.
The number of tender and devout minds who
have been fascinated by him is very many.
Of course those who have given themselves up
to him, as a friend of mine in the past did, to
be led and guided by him to the exclusion of
all other teachers, have no difficulty. They
accept him as a seer; as the greatest of all
great interpreters of life and its problems; as
infallible; as settling everything for them —
from him there is no appeal. Many others
who have made themselves familiar with his
works — the many, I might say — cannot take

that position. They admit his goodness as a
man, his greatness of mind, the marvelousness
of his nature. They admit him to be one of
the greatest of great psychologists. And if
in this chorus of voices my own whisper could
be heard, I should be inclined to say that
it is this wondrous psychological ability that
distinguishes Swedenborg above all modern
men — his ability of taking the interior ideas
of things, and of so living in and with what we
may call the spiritual essences of things that
they become to him objective realities. I know
how coldly such a suggestion as this would be
received by devout men who have taken
Swedenborg as their seer. When, however,
one reads Dante, one feels as if everything
were as real as when one reads Swedenborg.
The men and women remain in the mind as
individual, as vivid, as lifelike, as do Swedenborg's. It would seem as if Dante all but believed in the literalness of his descriptions of
places and people. But, says one, he wrote
poetry, and Swedenborg did not. The peculi-
arity about Swedenborg is his entire lack of the

strictly poetical. Emerson, remarking upon this lack, says : " His books have no melody, no emotion, no humor, no relief to the dead, prosaic level. The entire want of poetry in so transcendent a mind . . is a kind of warning." This is all the more remarkable as Swedenborg restored to the thought of the world the lost science of correspondencies. This science may be suggested in a few words to those who have no correct idea of what is meant by it. The idea is that the natural world is the outbirth of the spiritual world. Unseen evil is manifested in things hurtful and ugly; unseen good in things useful and beautiful. Man is a summary of nature; nature is man in diffusion; all things, therefore, in nature, in fire, air, earth, and water — every beast, bird, fish, insect, and reptile — every tree, herb, fruit, and flower, represent and correspond to things in the mind of man and in the spiritual world. The Scriptures are written according to this science of correspondence, and by aid of the science their mysteries are unlocked. There are, according to Swedenborg, three heavens,

consisting of three orders of angels; the first
distinguished for love, the second for wisdom,
and the last for obedience. All angels have
lived on earth; none were created such. They
are men and women in every respect. They
marry, and live in societies, in cities and coun-
tries, just as in this world, but in happiness
and glory ineffable. All in whom love is the
ruling motive are in the heavens; all in whom
self-love is the ruling motive are in hell — or
in one of three hells. If one spirit desires to
see another, the desire immediately brings
them together; there is no necessity to take a
long journey. Love attracts, hate repels and
separates. There is no obligation, as here, to
remain in any uncongenial society. There are
no artificial bonds. All is real, and according
to the interior fact. Thus the science of correspondencies runs through everything — all
orders, all societies. I confess to you that
about very much of this there is strong proba-
bility, and a kind of fascination. I have found
in reading Swedenborg's books that for a time
they have a charm, and one is carried along

from wonder to wonder, wishing it were all
true; but by and by it becomes mechanical.
It seems too ingenious. The very order becomes wearisome. It is like going into one of
those gardens in France where everything is
so neat and precise — trees all clipped to represent beasts, birds, and fishes, castles and
houses ; at first the newness charms, but after
a while you long to plunge into the forest to
escape it. In the forest there is just as much
order and law as in that garden, but it does not
obtrude itself upon you as the first thing. It
is hidden. The regnant idea is life, variety,
beauty, freedom. And yet in that forest not a
single law of creation is set at defiance. Everything moves as it was ordained to move.

No one can be more severely critical than
Emerson when he chooses, as he has an eye
keen enough to see where the defects come in.
While he does not to me suggest any explanation of this wonderful vision-power of Swedenborg, yet he sees where the defects are, as
when he says : " These angels that Swedenborg
paints give us no very high idea of their dis-

cipline and culture. They are all country par-
sons. Their heaven is a *fête champêtre,* an
evangelical picnic of French distribution of
prizes to virtuous peasants. Strange, scholas-
tic, didactic, passionless, bloodless man, who
denotes classes of souls as a botanist disposes
of a carex, and visits doleful hells as a stratum
of chalk or hornblende ! He has no sympathy. He goes up and down the world of
men, a modern Rhadamanthus in gold-headed
cane and peruke, and, with nonchalance and
the air of a referee, distributes souls. Swedenborg is disagreeably wise, and, with all his
accumulated gifts, paralyzes and repels." To
an extent that criticism is just, and yet it does
nothing further than create skepticism as to
the claims of this seer of Stockholm. It does
not account for him, or throw any light into
the deep mystery of this man's nature. Nega-
tive criticism is easy, but to offer an exegesis
of a great life crowded with remarkable facts
and events, so as to bring it into unity with
itself, is not so easy. We have to recognize
that it is not impossible that God might pre-

pare some man to whose mind he should reveal
something more about the life of man after
death has divested him of his material body.
This is not at all unlikely. It is not altogether
impossible that Swedenborg may have been
that man. I do not say that he is. If such
revelations were made, it is not impossible
that the revelations, and his own thoughts and
inferences from them, may have been so mixed
up and confused as that he should take the
one for the other; so that in these visions of
Swedenborg there may be fact and fiction in-
extricably combined. This is certain, that
many intelligent and devout people have derived great comfort from Swedenborg's revelations (as they hold them) of the spiritual
world. But that fact must not be made too
much of, speaking generally. Swedenborg's
doctrine of the spiritual body and of the spiritual world seems, in most particulars, so in
accord with St. Paul's setting forth of the
truths of immortality in that wonderful resur-
rection chapter in the First Epistle to the Cor-
inthian Christians, that the consolation may

come from the truth that is in it, and not from
anything that Swedenborg has added to it or
developed from it. For myself, I cannot see
what should hinder any of us from deriving
the same amount of comfort from that which
has been spoken by our Lord and his Apostles.
The comfort which the Christian mourner gets
respecting the loved and gone cannot be derived from the scenery of the surroundings in
which they are, nor from the companionships
in the midst of which they are; but from these
simple facts, that they are as much in God's
care and keeping as ever they were — are freed
from the pains and sorrows which belong to
this condition of life, and are happy in the
love and life God gives them. Add what else
you like, these are the true sources of comfort.
But, says a Swedenborgian to me, the spiritual
world is more real to me when I accept these
revelations of the seer.   I have often wondered
what is meant by that word " real," as so used.
Does it mean simply more materialized, or
what?

If we derive our comfort from anything

short of faith in the divine character as being in itself pure and perfect goodness and fatherliness, are we not relying on something external to God himself ? Have you not noticed the striking difference between the Lord and his Apostles and all other teachers in this respect, that they make all happiness to depend on inward states of heart, and not on external surroundings ? Put the man of perfectly regenerated soul where you will, the desert rejoices and blossoms as the rose at his coming. In this respect our Lord and his Apostles stand away and above all other teachers, in that they do not bribe men into goodness by the detailed picturings of any external heaven, and even when they speak of the loss which in eternity men out of harmony with God suffer, the retributive word is a word short, sharp, generic. There is no dwelling on hideous details. Not place, but condition ; not surroundings, but states of heart and mind — these with them are everything. Not what God can give, but what he is in himself — these are the thoughts which occupy them. In this respect they reach

the ideal of which the highest teachers have
spoken.

It would take up more of our space than
is allowable if I should attempt even the
most inadequate setting forth of the interpretations of Swedenborg. For he regards himself as an interpreter of Scripture, a seer into
the mysteries of God. His interpretations of
Scripture are not always such as seem to bring
Scripture into harmony with itself. One is
startled to find that, notwithstanding his devoutness, and his deep repentance after sin,
and his faith in God, King David is in hell ;
and much more taken aback to find Paul the
Apostle there too, and that because he taught
the doctrine of justification by faith, toward
which Swedenborg has much antipathy. When
we find these among the facts, it makes us
doubt the factuality of the facts. Moreover,
one cannot but doubt the correctness of the
testimony of Swedenborg when he tells us that
the Last Judgment took place in the spiritual
world in the year 1757. He tells us also that
the Dutch in the other world live in a heaven

by themselves, and the English in a heaven by themselves.   Not a few curiosities of this kind are to be found in his writings.

And yet, though we may seriously doubt the objectivity of his visions, or, if he had real visions, doubt his accuracy in reporting them ; though we may doubt also his correctness in expounding the nature of Jesus the Christ — making if I understand him aright, a kind of tabernacle in which God dwelt, affirming the divinity, but denying the perfect humanity — yet there is so much that commends itself as psychologic truth all up and down the writings of Swedenborg that it is impossible not to regard him as something more than a visionary — a great teacher to the world at large, as well as a great mystery.   For a very long time to come, perhaps always, he will be a study to men of succeeding generations.   Men will try to account for these visions of his on which his fame rests.   Psychologists and philosophers tell us that underneath man's ordinary consciousness is what has been called a subconsciousness, and that it is possible for men to sit apart from this sub-consciousness, and mistake the visions which arise in it for objective realities. In this way they try to account for the visions of Swedenborg. I do not undertake to affirm that such a method is adequate or satisfactory. The capabilities of human nature have never yet been measured, nor can they be in this limited condition where the material reveals and yet obstructs our perceptions. It is always best to hold ourselves in an attitude not too stiff and unelastic, and yet not too pliant or unconservative. God has put bones into our nature as well as given us flesh. The flesh yields while the bones remain firm. And so in every man there ought to be an ability of conservatism balanced by an ability of receiving impressions from everything good around us. We are admonished to " prove all things, and to hold fast that which is good." In Swedenborg there is a great deal that is undeniably good and great; there is very much which remains doubtful, problematical; to very many men, men too who are neither ignorant nor stupid, altogether unintelligible and unaccountable. So far as he is a commentator on the Christian Scriptures I should be disposed to consult him carefully; so far as he undertakes to go beyond the teachings of Christ and his Apostles I listen patiently, but in a condition of noncommittal; so far as he contradicts that teaching which to me is authoritative, because in its quality superior to anything else I can find, and in its evidence irresistible — so far I must regard him as wrong and untrustworthy. I cannot refuse, however, to recognize that, as Emerson says, "He elected goodness as the clue to which the soul must cling in all this labyrinth of nature. Nothing can keep you, not fate, nor health, nor admirable intellect — none can keep you but rectitude only, rectitude for ever and ever."

I cannot forget that he set Christ before men as the sole and only revelation of the nature of God. I cannot ignore the fact that his doctrine of the omnipresence of God's Spirit is beautiful and complete. "All things (he says), and each of them to the very utter-

most, exist and subsist instantly from God. If
the connection of anything with him were
broken for a moment, it would instantly vanish;
for existence is perpetual subsistence, and
preservation perpetual creation."

Swedenborg made no attempt to establish a
sect. He regarded the truth that had been
given to him as universal and for all who
could receive it. A sect has grown into form
which accepts his writings as nothing less than
revelations from heaven. Many of the men
who esteem him the most highly are not in
harmony with any movement which aims to
sectarianize his name and fame. The " New
Church signified by the New Jerusalem in the
Revelation " was organized in 1788 by Robert
Hindmarsh, a printer in Clerkenwell, London,
who was elected by lot to baptize and ordain
his comrades in the ministry. There are some
sixty small societies in Great Britain. But
the disciples of the Swedish seer are more
numerous in the United States than elsewhere.

It seems strange to us that so few people in
any church or sect seem willing to allow the

all-sufficiency of Scripture truth as adequate to
the enlightenment of the mind of man in regard to the faith and duty which God requires
of us in this brief life. Something must be
added. If you inquire diligently into the controversies of the Church, you will find almost
invariably that it is the something added
which is the bone of contention. Of course, if
I could believe that Swedenborg was the last
and greatest of the seers I should have to be his
humble disciple. To me that conviction is impossible. One wonders, however, if the time
will ever come when men will be able to trust
solely and alone in the teaching of Jesus Christ
and his Apostles, and in the gift of the Holy
Spirit as the great interpreter. In the midst
of all the varied ecclesiasticisms of our day we
must not allow ourselves to forget that for
that first three hundred years in which wonders
were wrought men had only the manuscript
records of the life of Christ and the apostolical
Epistles. They had no formularies outside of
these of which we have any trace. Not till
some time during the fifth century did the

Apostles' Creed — that model of simplicity —
take its final form. The other simple creed
called the Nicene was not in form till near the
beginning of the fourth century. For three
hundred years or more there were no authoritative documents added to the Gospels and
Epistles. With these, Christian teachers and
preachers did their great work in the face of a
hostile paganism and a degraded heathenism.
All other additions everywhere have grown up
since then. One wonders why that which was
all-sufficient in the martyr-days of Christen-
dom is not sufficient now. Every man has the
liberty to depart from the simplicities of Scripture — to add to those early Christian documents or take from them — but one may be
pardoned for holding the belief that the more
faithfully we adhere to the old apostolic conditions the nearer we are to the mind of Christ
and the heart of God.

VII.

HORACE BUSHNELL.

WHEN, in the summer of the year 1874,
a three months' vacation was granted
me that I might visit the United States, I
wrote to my friend the Rev. G. W. Field, of
Bangor, that there were two things essential,
and all other things optional and to be deter-
mined by possibility and convenience. The
two essential things were that I should see
Niagara and Dr. Bushnell. Such a request
may seem peculiar and need some explanation.
To me Niagara was the greatest natural fact
in all America, and to me Dr. Bushnell, of
Hartford, was the man who of all men in
America had done my mind most service. On
my arrival I found that my friend had so ar-

ranged it that we were to go direct to Niagara and spend a week there ; then I was to preach in the pulpit of the South Church in Hartford for two Sabbaths, in order that I might have a full and fair opportunity of seeing and talking with Bushnell. During that week I was very lonesome and homesick, and the ability of seeing Bushnell some part of every day was the only adequate compensation I had. Alone in a hotel, all faces strange, in a strange land, did not suit my temperament at all. However, when I got through with my visit I left Hartford with something of regret, never expecting to see the city again, and certainly never expecting again to look on the face of the man who had to me been so very interesting. During that week I made discoveries which were surprising and painful.

Before I refer to them it may be as well to indicate why to see Bushnell had been one of the essential things in my visit to this side of the ocean. There were days in my early ministry when doubt and faith struggled together in death grapple. Two subjects trou-

bled me exceedingly : one, the nature of the
personality of Jesus ; the other, the subject of
miracles — especially the latter. Talking one
day to a ministerial friend, a man of exquisitely
refined mind and broad culture, he asked me if
I had read a book recently imported from
America, entitled "Nature and the Supernatural." Very soon I was occupied in reading that
book. To me it was a wonderful book, and so
adapted to my then condition of mind that if
God had sent an angel from heaven to me with
a message of deliverance from doubt, it could
not have been more thoroughly adapted to my
state. I had previously read a volume of sermons by this same author, entitled "Sermons
for the New Life," and they struck me as being
very remarkable for their devoutness and spiritual force. I think that from the day I read
that book on "Nature and the Supernatural "
to the present hour I have had no doubts on
the personality of Jesus, and no skepticism on
the subject of the miracles recorded in the
New Testament, worth notice. Now, when any
one has done for your mind as much as Bush-

nell did for mine, you will owe him a debt of gratitude which you can never pay. So much for the reason why I specially desired to see Dr. Bushnell.

Well, some one may ask, and what kind of a man did you find ? With a delicacy which is characteristic of him, my friend in Bangor had written me to this effect : " You must not be surprised if you are a little disappointed in Dr. Bushnell personally. He has been a sufferer for twenty years, is very much of an invalid, and, if he does not take to people, is rather impatient and somewhat unamiable ; but it is disease, and not the natural disposition of the man." So that I was prepared to find Bushnell a kind of wreck of his once brilliant self. But I was most agreeably disappointed. The worn frame was there; the traces of suffering were there. He characterized himself as among the " vestiges of creation." But there was no mental feebleness. Every day for a week I saw him some part of the day. There would be a difference in his days. He had his good and bad days, as is the case

with all invalids suffering as he was. But to
me he was so amiable and good, so considerate
and kind, so simple, so modest, yet so vigorous
mentally, so manly, so beautiful in spirit, that
among the memories of my life which have for
me a perpetual charm that visit to Bushnell
is one.

The discovery that I made when in Hartford
which to me was very surprising and painful
was that Bushnell was regarded as something
of a heretic, and that there had been an attempt
to bring him before his ecclesiastical association
for trial on the charge of heterodoxy. To hear
from his own lips that if I wanted to be on the
best of terms with strictly orthodox brethren
it would be as well not to make too generous
reference to my esteem for himself was to me
exceedingly painful. I remember replying
with some warmth that, much as I lacked, I
hoped that I was not craven and mean enough
to refuse to acknowledge my indebtedness to
him for the removal of doubts which, if they
had grown, would have silenced my voice as a
minister forever, or have taken me into the

ranks of rationalists.   One of our most revered
ministers, the Rev. Dr. Buckingham, of Spring-
field, a man whose orthodoxy has never had
any suspicion cast upon it, says that Dr. Bushnell was " the rarest genius and most suggestive
preacher that for forty years ever occupied the
pulpit among Congregationalists."   I came to
America from a country where it was a very
rare thing indeed to meet with a minister of
any standing among Presbyterians, Congregationalists and Baptists who was not thoroughly familiar with Bushnell's writings.   I
remember how the tears ran down the old
man's face when I told him this.   He had remarked to me that a London publisher, unso-
licited, and on whom he had no claim, had
sent him two thousand dollars ; when I replied
that if said publisher had sent him ten thousand dollars he would have approached nearer
the line of honesty, it seemed incredible to him.
" Why, Dr. Bushnell," I remarked, " there is
no man in America read more generally by intelligent laymen, as well as ministers, in England than you are."   He seemed incredulous,

but I saw his lip tremble and his nostril quiver, and I knew he felt deeply moved by the fact — for a fact it was. When I wrote in English papers of my interviews with Bushnell, and my impressions of him, there was intense interest excited, and on my return there were more questions asked about Bushnell than about almost any other subject.

In pursuing this subject, I will give you, first of all, my impressions of Bushnell personally, and then I will refer, of course very briefly, to his principal books — books which probably would never have been written but for that invalidism of twenty-five years which laid him aside from all active pastoral work.

As to his personality, Bushnell impressed me as a man of sublime courage — a man of what the old prophets would have called "vision." He did not reason out truth, like a man inferring that the sun shines because he sees light on his path, but he saw the sun — he saw the truth. Not that which we have inferred from other things, but "that which we have seen and heard declare we unto you" was the atti-

tude of his mind. I think that I never met a
man who seemed to have so little between him
and Christ. His love to Christ and his simple
trust in him was peculiar. He had no more
doubt that when he was let loose from this
body he would go direct to Christ than a little
child has when let loose from school that it
will go straight home to its mother. He felt
that he should know Christ the moment he set
eyes upon him — that there was such love between them that they could not mistake one
another. I came away from my visit to Bushnell saying to myself, " There is a man who
believes in Christ more than he believes in anything or anybody."

Another beautiful feature in his character
was the fact that on the shadier side of seventy
years of age he was as much a learner in the
school of Christ, as much a disciple, as when
young. His mind had not in the least become
fixed, set, or fossilized. Now, it seems to me
that this is one of the infallible signs of character of the purest and genius of the highest
order. Have you never remarked the arrange-

ment of that string of benefits which is drawn
out before our eyes in the one hundred and
third Psalm: "Bless the Lord, O my soul, and
forget not all his benefits: who forgiveth all
thine iniquities; who healeth all thy diseases;
who redeemeth thy life from destruction; who
crowneth thee with loving-kindness and tender
mercies; who satisfieth thy mouth with good
things, so that thy youth is renewed like the
eagle's"? The administration of the Spirit of
God to the spirit of man results in the perpetual renewal of youth. The second part of
Bushnell's book on "Vicarious Sacrifice," entitled "Forgiveness and Law," had just come
into his hands when I saw him.

That book, "Forgiveness and Law," was
intended to be a revision of the last part of
"Vicarious Sacrifice." I asked him whether
he considered these two books as final on that
theme. "No; not at all," he replied; "they
are only suggestions. If I had more light to-
morrow I would recall them both, or supersede
them. That is the only truthful and devout
attitude of a human mind." He believed that

God was working all the time on the human mind, and that when a man deserved more light he would get it. Use what you have, and you will get more. He did not scruple to express his contempt for a man who had not the courage of his convictions. Men who were playing with truth, or flirting with it, he did not spare. He would have gone to the stake himself for what he believed rather than abandon it or seem to be unfaithful to it, and he had no kind of respect for the weakness of men less true to the light that was in him. I believe that he did more to prevent rationalism getting a footing in the State of Connecticut than any one has any idea of. Whether we agree with a man or not, let us try to be fair to him. Let us willingly own his power and recognize his worth. How strange that people were afraid of this man — afraid of him because they did not understand him !

The tenth chapter of Bushnell's "Nature and the Supernatural," entitled "The Character of Jesus Forbids his Possible Classification among Men," did more to prevent our theologi-

cal students and thinking laymen in England
from moving in the Rationalistic direction
than any other volume or any score of volumes.
Bushnell's influence on England has been immense, and it has been beneficial, especially
with young men at that period when, beginning to think for themselves, they are in
danger of moving toward that which seems
most captivating, but is not profound. There
has never appeared in America a man who
answered Theodore Parker so completely as
did Bushnell. I have personally great respect
for Theodore Parker's courage, his benevolence,
his faithfulness to the cause of the outcast;
but his theological thinking is certainly not of
a high order, and misleading. Yet he had
force and power, and was a great controversial-
ist. But it is pretty poor controversy which
simply decries a man and says he is dangerous.
The only respectable way of controversy, the
only reputable and Christian way, is to meet
inferior thought with superior thought. If a
man's light is only moonshine, pour sunshine
into his mind. If a man's stick is crooked,

put a straight stick by the side of it. If a man's ideal of the nature of God or man is inferior, put the higher and nobler and purer idea by the side of it. In the long run, that is the only way you can get victory, and it is the only way in which victory ought to be won. Every now and again, it seems to me, when we are in danger of putting that which has been said, and even put into formulas, about Christ between ourselves and Christ, giving it an undue influence over us, God in his providence raises up some man who, in his faith in Christ and his love for him, surpasses all but the choicest and meekest of his generation ; and this man, whose Christliness no one can justly deny, does not view truths exactly as we do, but explores them and lets new light into them. And God does this for our sakes, in order that our vision may not be fixed on the shadow of Christ, but only on Christ himself. Bushnell was so confident in his own sincerity and in the worth of those opinions which made him seem to think differently from some of his brethren, that he could

say, "If what I am about to say should be
stifled and killed by an over-hasty judgment,
it will yet rise again the third day. This feeling I have, not in exultation, it seems to me,
not so much in the shape of defiance as in the
shape of consolation — a soft whisper that
lingers round me in my studies, to hold me firm
and to smooth me into an even, uncaring spirit.
Still, the best of all attitudes I know is this :
Let me do the right, and let God take care of
me. I want to be in no better hands." Controversy among brethren ought never to have
about it the spirit and flavor of contention for
the mastery. Men should ask themselves always such serious questions as these : What
good am I about to seek by this controversy ?
How will the unrenewed and unchurched men
of society regard it ? Will it do them good or
evil ? Will it incline them to listen more at-
tentively to the voice of the Church, or will it
supply them with yet another argument for
aloofness from and hostility toward those who,
by their manifest love of one another, are
Christ's disciples ? "By this shall all men

know that ye are my disciples, if ye have love
one to another." I am surprised oftentimes at
the recklessness shown by men as to the effect
which certain courses of conduct will have
upon men of the world — men whom every
sincere Christian wants to win for Christ and
his church. But men ought ever to ask themselves the question, What good am I going to
do by this course? And if the good be doubtful even, it is best to let it alone. I think with
good Dr. Buckingham, that it would have been
nothing short of a calamity if so eminent a
genius as Dr. Bushnell had been driven out of
fellowship with the brethren whom he loved
and ardently desired to assist in everything
which pertained to the kingdom of God.

Let me refer briefly to his books.

His sermons on "The New Life" are such
as only he himself could have preached. "Nature and the Supernatural" is perhaps his
greatest book. In it he deals with theology,
with pantheism, with naturalism, and shows
how nature is not a system in itself, but needs
the supernatural to complete it. He takes up

the fact of sin, and the consequences of sin, and shows how this world was anticipatively adapted to the training, not of perfect men, but of sinning men. He shows, further, that there is no remedy in development or self-reformation. Then he goes on to show how God governs the world by a supernatural method — and yet not against law, as the objectors say, but by the bringing higher supernatural laws to the control of the lower or natural laws. Then he opens his great tenth chapter on the superhuman personality of Christ, and shows how great a matter it is that one such character has lived in the world. He speaks of miracles in such a way as to make one perceive that they are in entire harmony with what went before; that Jesus Christ is the greatest miracle of all, and that it is impossible to reject the miracles he did without also rejecting him — a fact which experience but too often verifies.

Several volumes of sermons have been given to the press, all aglow with thought and feeling. The book on " Vicarious Sacrifice," and

that (supplementary to it) on "Forgiveness
and Law," are suggestive, but not so satisfactory on the themes discussed as one would
wish, and as he himself felt. Books entitled
" Building Eras " and " Work and Play " contain essays of his on their various themes that
are of very special worth. A letter of his to
the Pope, in one of these, is a curiosity in
literature. A singularly original book on
" Woman Suffrage," entitled " Reform against
Nature," would be excellent for all women in-
fected with a desire to be politicians.

But of all useful books for our age, I am inclined to give " Christian Nurture " almost the
front place. That such a book should be neg-
lected by fathers and mothers and churches
is a sign that to have light given is not by any
means the same as to have received light.

There is a recently published " Pastoral
Letter of the House of Bishops," in which
the representatives of the Episcopal Church
warn men of the consequences of the present
condition of things in this land as regards
family life and the neglect of Christian nur-

ture in families. It is a long while since I
read a document so satisfactory as far as its
practical suggestions are concerned. Now,
no man has treated this theme so wisely and
with so much philosophic insight as Bushnell. No one of any judgment and intelligence can take objection to anything advanced
in "Christian Nurture." I believe that the
most dangerous form of atheism in this land is
not that which on platforms denies God's sovereignty and man's responsibility for anything
but the free exercise of his animal powers,
although that is dangerous enough, God knows
— tending to multiply Anarchists and Com-
munists, already too numerous. The most
dangerous form of atheism is that which lurks
in the family, emasculating and counteracting
God's law as given on the page of revelation.
In the last book of the New Testament the
kind of wickedness which should devastate
and desolate the earth is called "the mystery
of lawlessness." No law anywhere — no law
in the family, no law in the Church, no law in
the nation, or only such as can be successfully

trampled on and set at defiance. Repudiate
the Divine Sovereignty, and then man's sovereignty is without adequate foundation.
Atheism in the administration of family life is
certain to bring with it that which the prophet
Daniel calls " the abomination which maketh
desolate." I commend to all fathers and
mothers Bushnell's book on " Christian Nurture " as pure gold.

I must not omit one of his most thoughtful
books, entitled " Moral Uses of Dark Things."
What insight that book displays ! In it he
treats of such themes as these : " Of Night
and Sleep," " Of Want and Waste," " Of Bad
Government," " Of Physical Pain," " Of Non-
Intercourse between Worlds," " Of Things
Unsightly and Disgusting," "Of Plague and
Pestilence," " Of Insanity," " Of the Mutabili-
ties of Life," and other themes. It is a book
full of windows — windows through which
one looks into a wide, wide area of thought
and speculation. Bushnell was emphatically
a thinker. He would not be called a scholar
in the sense of a man who had scraped to-

gether and stored up in his memory the
thoughts of others, but his mind was alive
all the time, and thought poured into it and
then out of it again in new and beautiful
forms.

I think that I never felt so ashamed of
preaching as when, on that second Sunday I
spent at Hartford, Bushnell sat in the pew before me and I had him for an auditor. It
seemed to me that absurdity could no further
go than that I should preach and Bushnell
should listen. And that Sunday morning after
service we walked together through that park
which he had been the means of inducing the
city of Hartford to undertake to make. The
whole region used to be a place of refuse, and
the brook that skirts it, now clear and sweet,
a stream into which boys threw kittens and
everything else they could. As he was dying,
the city authorities unanimously voted to call
it Bushnell Park, and the old man knew before
he went hence that that was to be its name.
Crowned with the marble State House, it is
now a thing of beauty — a joy forever! I

shall not forget that morning walk, and the
tenderness of the man, and what he said to me
about preaching; I shall not forget very soon
how he looked and how he spoke as he talked
of his books. "These that are uttered," he
said, "do not trouble me. It is that within
which I cannot utter which troubles me."
And when I looked into those eyes with that
far-away look in them, so seldom seen, but
once seen never forgotten, I could well believe
that there was much in him which he could
not get uttered. The feelings and thoughts
of the soul were too great for language. That
morning he said "good-by" to me, and added,
so quietly and with such gentle pathos in his
voice, "Well, my brother, I am glad to have
been well enough to see you so much this
week; glad to know you — I suppose we shall
never meet again until we get to the other
side." In February, 1876, he went home; went
home with a benediction on his lips. Very
slowly, and with pauses intermingled — for he
was very weak — he said: "Well, now, we are
all going home together; and I say, the Lord

be with you, and in grace and peace and love — and that is the way I have come along home." It was his dying benediction, spoken out of the almost sleep and exhaustion of his mind.

"God spared his life till all men were at peace with him." For myself, I am of opinion that the day has not even yet dawned, except among those who knew him personally and intimately, in which ample justice can be done to the genius of Horace Bushnell. He was too original to be understood at first, and by men and women accustomed to assume that Bible truths could only be expressed in one form of words. Knowing nothing of him but what his books revealed, England did him ampler justice than he has ever here received. English Nonconformists are given to speak out their thoughts without restraint, yet I never once heard the orthodoxy of Bushnell impugned. Men there are accustomed to consider a man orthodox enough who exalts Christ and holds on to the inspired records faithfully. They never find that that kind of man does anything but good. However, for myself I owe him a great deal; a great deal of love and reverence for the light he gave me on themes which were to me very dark. And what higher thing can one man do for another than this?

What baser ingratitude could there be than for a man not to own the man whom God employed as a light-bearer to his soul? Professor Phelps says of him, after spending a time with him: "He was one of God's seers. He was commissioned to paint the vision precisely as he saw it on the Mount. The reception of it by other minds was their affair, not his. When I came near to the inner spirit of the man, it was beautifully and profoundly Christlike, if that of uninspired man ever was." So said all who, I believe, knew him well.

As the days go on, and as we ourselves become more Christlike in spirit, we shall find that there have been among the New England clergy few men of whom Christian brethren have more cause to be proud, for whom they have more cause to be thankful, than the man of all men best known among the citizens of Hartford, the bright and brilliant genius, the sincere disciple, the passionate lover of his Lord — Horace Bushnell.

VIII.

FREDERICK DENISON MAURICE.

ONE is apt to assume that men whom we ourselves know with some degree of thoroughness must necessarily be well known by others. I was very thoroughly awakened to the idea that this is not so when, speaking recently to a lady and gentleman who move among the cultured people of the old city of the Puritans, they told me, with evident sincerity and honesty, that they had never heard the name of Frederick Denison Maurice. This fact set me thinking. Here is a name that has appeared in reviews, magazines and newspapers — specially religious newspapers — quite frequently for the last fifty years; a man whose inner life and whose relations to men have been set forth very elaborately in two biographical volumes; a man who was the author of some thirty books on topics relating to theology and metaphysics — and yet quite respectable, and to a degree cultured people may never have heard of him. In the case to which I refer the lady and gentleman belonged to a denomination in which F. D. Maurice is seldom, I apprehend, quoted as anything of an authority, or seldom at all — because, being born into that denomination, his father being a minister therein, he soon worked his way out of it, he and his mother and his sisters, leaving the poor old father absolutely alone, in what appeared to them a land-locked harbor, into which no ships came with merchandise from afar, while mother, son and daughters set sail on wider, if more tempestuous waters. I confess to feeling much of sympathy and much of sadness for the position of that old Unitarian minister when his wife and every member of his family deserted the church of which he was minister because they could no longer feel that the truth as to God and the human soul was there. Fancy the state of feeling into which that father must have been thrown when one morning he received this note from one of his daughters, in her sister's name as well as in her own : " We do not think it consistent with the duty we owe to God to attend a Unitarian place of worship," and further states that she cannot any longer consent to take the communion with him ! The reply of the father is brief, but one can feel the heavings of his heart and see the tears as they drop on the paper :

My Dear Anne :
The sensation your letter has excited in my mind is beyond my powers to describe. I am totally unable to answer it. May God enable me to perform my duty ! I certainly was unprepared for such a stroke. I should have been thankful if any previous intimation had been given. I have not acted as a father to whom no confidence ought to be shown. Nor have I refused to argue or state my reasons of belief in such a way as might have apprised me somewhat of what I expect from those who are dearer to me than they can imagine. But if ever they are parents they may then conceive the distress of

                                    M. Maurice.

All the members of the Maurice household were noted for two things — their perfect purity of feeling and their bright, keen intelligence. The subject of our brief essay seems to have been a saint from childhood. His cousin, Dr. Goodeve, the one companion of his boyhood who survives him, writes : " During our intercourse as boys I never knew him to commit even an ordinary fault, or apparently to entertain an immoral idea. He was the gentlest, most docile and affectionate of creatures ; but he was equally earnest in what he believed to be right, and energetic in the pursuit of his views. It may be thought an extravagant assertion, a mere formal tribute to a deceased friend and companion, but, after a long and intimate experience of the world, I can say, with all sincerity, that he was the most saintlike individual I have ever met — Christlike, if I dare to use the word ! "

His companions in boyhood have left the testimony that " he never said an unkind word nor did an unfeeling or ungenerous action to his companions ; yet he was untiring in work in

and out of study hours, thus easily surpassing
his schoolfellows, yet without any assumption
of superiority over them." People are too apt
to assume that great men develop out of bad,
ungovernable boys, and that great thinkers are
sure to have some terrible elements of disorder
in their make-up. This man of whom I am
writing is the clergyman concerning whom
so eminent an individual as John Stuart Mill
(whose whole up-bringing had been such as
to create prejudice against all clergymen) is
recorded to have remarked that there was
one clergyman of his acquaintance "who had
brains enough and to spare."

The word "saint" has become so associated
with a feminine or with a " goody-goody " idea
of character, that it may be useful and refresh-
ing to us to meet with a man in modern times
whom everybody personally acquainted with
him acknowledged to be saintlike and Christlike in character, whatever they thought of
his opinions, who was Platonic in intellect — a
theological Socrates in these recent years. I
believe that the very highest order of intel-

lectual greatness demands also as its counterpart the very highest order of goodness.

There cannot be a doubt that the influence of Maurice's writings on some of the choicest minds of the age, both in England and America, has been exceedingly powerful and salutary. When men like Dean Stanley and Charles Kingsley and many others hardly less celebrated call him master, it is idle talk to speak slightingly of him and say that he is too mystical ever to be popular or influential. No record of modern thinkers in the church is, or can be at all complete which ignores the man whom Mr. Gladstone has called a "spiritual splendor" — although Mr. Gladstone confesses that Maurice's order of mind is a kind of enigma to him. Others have felt the same. So celebrated a writer as the late Principal Tulloch, of Scotland, remarks how needful it is to study his writings to get an initial clue with which to begin. "Even with such a clue his marvelous subtlety is often evasive; without it, it is hopeless to read a coherent meaning into his several writings and controversies."

So that one would assume that Maurice could never have been a popular preacher, which is true. A teacher of teachers must necessarily have, as his first audience — the audience to which he speaks *viva voce* — a very limited number of people. It was so with Maurice. But, happily, there were publishers ready to take and print almost every thing he produced, and his books found a sufficient number of readers, subtle as they were, to sell several editions of most of them, and the number of readers among clergymen is steadily increasing all the time. My own interest in him was aroused by an Episcopal clergyman who became the most intimate clerical friend I ever had in this world. He was some fifteen years my senior in age, and we did not see alike on ecclesiastical or theological themes, but our mental disagreements seemed to have no ability to keep us apart. Every week we were together, generally on Mondays and Saturdays, he studying for his Sunday preaching at one desk and I at another in the same room. The world has never

seemed the same to me since that man left it.
And he had such unbounded reverence for
Maurice that I could not help being interested
in the man, though my prejudices against
Maurice were very strong. He seemed to me
so misty and mystical. I labored at him and
failed to understand him. And yet I felt what
a magnificent mind it was with which I was
laboring. He reminded me of Plato, and of
Hegel. Many a time I had the opportunity
of hearing him preach, and stupidly refrained
from going near him. I ought to have known
that a man who had such magnetic influence
over others must have had in him something
out of the common, and I ought to have con-
quered my prejudices.

Once my friend and I went together to the
Workingmen's College in London, of which
Maurice was the founder. He was to speak
to the men of that college — men of the respectable artisan class, who spent their even-
ings there studying and improving themselves.
Their appreciation of their founder showed
itself in the crowd which filled the hall —

every foot of room being occupied. Suddenly there slipped into the room a man about middle height, of most modest demeanor, and all eyes were turned to him. When he rose to speak the applause was spontaneous and hearty to a degree. What a beautiful face it was, to be sure! I had heard of "the angel-faced Maurice," but no photographic portrait seemed to indicate why. And I saw at once that the face could not be photographed. You must catch the expression as the man was speaking, or it would be of no use. And herein the immense superiority of oil painting comes out — the true artist catches the expression and gives the life. The sun has no personality in him, and cannot deal with personality — only with hard lines and light and shade. The best faces can never be photographed — faces with spiritual light in them, as if something were shining through them.

Such was the face of Maurice as I saw him on that occasion. He spoke with great hesitancy; but every word seemed to tell, every word seemed saturated with soul. I was afraid he would stop. There was something in the man and in his voice which held you. When we left I reproached myself: "Fool that you are, never to have heard this man before when you had had the opportunity!"

He was then living at Cambridge (Professor of Moral Philosophy), and had come up to London for a season. I resolved to go whenever I saw the name of Maurice announced anywhere, if it were possible. We spoke to him after the address, and the way in which he held my friend's hand in both his and unconsciously stroked it as he spoke to him, was very significant.

The next time we went together, called by the announcement of the name of Maurice, was a very different occasion, yet not long after that on which we had listened to his voice at the Workingmen's College. It was by the side of the grave in Highgate Cemetery where the mortal investiture of this immortal spirit was committed to the tomb. It was a simple funeral, for every one knew how averse Maurice was to display. But it was a remark-

able gathering. Tennyson was expected, but
at the last moment could not come. Carlyle
had begun to grow feeble, and dared not
expose himself to the bleak winds of April.
There were crowds lining the roads to the
cemetery, and around the grave were men who
seldom, if ever, all met together before — certainly would never meet together again.

Next to me was the tall form of Charles
Kingsley, and then the slight figure of Dean
Stanley; a little farther off, the hard-lined,
thoughtful face of James Martineau, who in
controversy had grappled, not very successfully, with him who was gone. Then came
good Dr. Alexander Raleigh, whom, with Dr.
Vaughan, the Congregational Union of England and Wales sent over here immediately
after the Civil War as their representatives;
and near by was a Baptist clergyman of repute,
who, when I was introduced, said, "What a
meeting-place this is to day!" "I had no
idea you were an admirer of Maurice," I remarked. His reply was very significant:
"He gave me back the Gospel."

It may seem entirely out of the natural order of things to speak in the middle of an essay, of a man's funeral, but sometimes personal reminiscences prepare the mind to be interested in the teaching. And while I am writing of Maurice's funeral, it may be justifiable if I record a simple fact in relation to the funeral of the friend to whom I have referred, through whom my attention was called to the exceptional greatness and goodness of the man whom he all but worshiped.

He had said to his family : " When I die let my remains lie as close to those of Maurice as you can possibly get them." This sacred request was singularly provided for. When my friend's wife went to Highgate Cemetery to select the site of the grave, she mentioned her husband's wish. An available lot was discovered some hundreds of yards away. On her return she received a note from the registrar of the cemetery running thus : " By some unaccountable mistake, the lot next to that where repose the remains of the Rev. F. D. Maurice has been overlooked, and is unappropriated."

And so side by side the remains of the master and his disciple lie, their dust mingling in
death as their thoughts and loves had mingled
in life. It seems that sometimes Divine
Providence arranges for the gratification of the
deep heart-wishes of those who are entire believers in it, in a most peculiar way, as in
this case. The dearest and last wish of this
faithful disciple of Maurice was thus granted.

As is recorded in the biography of Maurice
by his son : " As soon as he (whose teachings
had been the subject of a great deal of controversy while he lived) was dead, there followed, both in the pulpit and in the press,
such a burst of grateful recognition of the
national services he had rendered as fairly
staggered numbers who had never heard his
name before, or had known him only under
false conceptions of him. It was said to me
by more than one man at the time that the
spontaneity and universality of the feeling
was so marked that there did not seem to
them to have been anything like it in England
since the Duke of Wellington's death. It was

the more remarkable because at the moment
scarcely a single notice came from his immediate friends. The blow to them had been too
stunning to admit of anything but silence."

It may now be necessary to say what con-
stituted Maurice a teacher of teachers, and of
what nature his teaching was. His basis
doctrine was that God had been revealed in
Christ as the Father of the spirit of man — of
man everywhere ; out of this grew everything
in his teaching. He believed that this revelation was distinct and clear in the teaching of
Jesus Christ, and that man's ignorance of the
fact, or his ignoring the fact, or repudiating the
fact made no difference to the fact. If a man
believes that the earth is flat it does not alter
the fact that it is round. One who had heard
him repeat in public the Lord's Prayer writes :
" No one who ever heard Maurice read the
Lord's Prayer can possibly forget it. The intensity of his convictions in the pulpit made his
message seem as luminous and clear as it was
brief and concentrated, though his teaching
had by no means the same character."

I know how difficult it is to accept the
teaching which seems to be that of the first
two words of the Lord's Prayer, and aver that
in their spirits all men are the children of
God. I know how much is involved in it.
So very many of the facts of life seem to
militate against it. Maurice would ask, " Is
it right to teach every child the Lord's
Prayer? Yes or no. If yes, then the first
two words contain the greatest of all revelations. If no, then our Lord ought to have
limited this word ' our ' in some way or
other."

Out of this view of the Fatherhood in God
over human spirits arose consistently Maurice's
principle of "universal redemption." No man
ever so emphatically and resolutely proclaimed
the greatness and completeness of the Atonement as wrought by Christ. He stood without any, even the slightest reservation on the
text, " God was in Christ reconciling the world
unto himself, not imputing their trespasses
unto them."

In a letter to his mother he sets forth the

view he held with an earnestness that is unmistakable. Perhaps that letter will help you to perceive how free from that timidity which characterizes most of us in our statements as to the extent and worth of the Atonement he is. "Now, my dearest mother," he writes, "you wish or long to believe yourself in Christ, but you are afraid to do so, because you think there is some experience that you are in him necessary to warrant that belief. Now, if any man, or an angel from heaven preach this doctrine to you, let him be accursed. You have this warrant for believing yourself in Christ, that you cannot do one loving act, you cannot obey one of God's commandments, you cannot pray, you cannot hope, you cannot love, if you are not in him. . . . What, then, do I assert? Is there no difference between the believer and unbeliever? Yes; the greatest difference. But the difference is not about the fact, but precisely in the belief of the fact. God tells us, 'In him (that is, in Christ) I have created all things, whether they be in heaven or on earth. Christ is the

head of every man.' Some men believe this
— some men disbelieve it. Those men who
disbelieve it walk after the flesh. They do
not believe that they are joined to the Almighty Lord of life, One who is mightier
than the world, the flesh and the Devil; One
who is nearer to them than their own flesh.
. . . But though tens of hundreds of
thousands of men so live, we are forbidden by
Christian truth to call this the real state of
any man. The truth is that every man is in
Christ; the condemnation of every man is
that he will not own the truth, he will not
act as if it were true that except he were
joined to Christ he could not think, breathe,
live, a single hour."

Another feature in Maurice's teaching was
the tremendous honor which he put on the
Scriptures. His interpretation of them was
often different from that adopted in his day,
but he exalted them above all other religious
writings as infinitely wiser and infinitely more
advanced in thought. He was brought up as
a child and youth in a system where the

opinions of men were made much of, and when
he came to the Scriptures it was a deliverance
to him, and he seemed to breathe the air of
freedom. His soul sprang into a new liberty,
like a chick breaking the shell, and getting on
to the copious acreage of the broad earth.
He used to say that there was nothing
specially difficult to him in the Scriptures,
nothing that he could not see a reason for,
except the destruction of the children who
went to cry out after the prophet. That he
always shrank from. But, as one has said,
"perhaps the young persecutors would have
grown up only to be incorrigibly bad men, and
it was a mercy to arrest them in their wickedness while young."

A third thing characteristic of Maurice was
his passionate desire for unity among Christians. He was haunted all his life, he says,
by this desire. "I would wish to live and
die," he writes, "for the assertion of this
truth: that the universal church is as much a
reality as any particular nation is; that the
church is the witness for the true constitution

of man as man, a child of God, an heir of
heaven, and taking up his pardon by baptism ;
that the world is a miserable, accursed, rebel-
lious order, which denies this foundation,
which will create a foundation of self-will,
choice, taste, opinion ; that in the world there
can be no communion; that in the church
there can be universal communion — communion in one body by one spirit."

Another aspect of Maurice's character was
that of a social reformer. He could not pass
through this world simply as a literary man
and a theologian. When gazing once on the
picture of the Last Supper by Leonardo da
Vinci, he complained of the smooth, girlish,
and sentimental face of John as being out of
keeping with the character of the man. Mr.
Kingsley who was with him, asked him why.
And he answered, " Why ? Was not St. John
the Apostle of Love ? When in such a world
of hate and misery as this, do you not think
that he had more furrows in his cheeks than
all the other Apostles ? " " And," says Kingsley, " I looked upon the furrows in that most

delicate yet most noble face, and knew that he spoke truth — of St. John and of himself likewise — and understood better from that moment what was meant by bearing the sorrows and carrying the infirmities of men."

Every man in his own order — and when Maurice began to ask himself in what direction he could move most usefully, he thought of the Workingmen's College, and of teaching men co-operation with one another. He was, too, the founder of Queen's College for the higher education of young women ; and of the " Girls' Home," a kind of industrial school for girls who, from the evil influences in their own homes, would be likely to fall into a vagrant way of life. He persuaded the ladies of his congregation to found this school, and give girls a thorough apprenticeship in household work — lessons in the business of the housemaid, the parlormaid, and the cook, and in all kinds of plain needlework, combined with lessons in reading, writing, arithmetic, singing, together with education in the Scriptures — which lessons he thought would be more prized and better remembered when associated with a school which aimed to give a preparation for the practical duties of life. " Every congregation," he says, " which meets to worship God and to join in communion seems pledged to do something for the neighborhood in which it is placed."

Men were somewhat afraid of him, because he did not repudiate, but rather accepted the name of a " Christian Socialist." He felt that if Christian clergymen would put themselves in right relations to the people, and do it in Christ's name and spirit, the people would follow them and be guided by them. " Then and always throughout life he looked upon it as essential to the cause of the poor that they should learn the impotence of lawlessness and riot," and that they should be so instructed as to win what they had a right to by reason and intelligence, and by no baser methods. But he held that anything would be better for England than that it should degenerate into a nation of mere moneygetters. No one knew better than he that every nation reaps what it

sows, and that if the people became riotous
and mutinous it would be because the more
intelligent and better circumstanced people had failed to do their duty to them, and
had been occupied selfishly about their own
concerns.

Among other efforts of his to diffuse truth,
he caused to be published for a time a paper
called " Politics for the People," but he could
give very little personal supervision, and the
paper never grew to what it might have been.
Many strifes between employers and employed
were appeased by his influence, or by the
kindly intervention of those who looked to
him as their leader.

I think that Maurice will come to be es-
teemed more and more as a great Christian
philosopher. He regarded everything in the
light of certain admitted principles. Until he
got to the divine ground of things and thoughts
he was restless and dissatisfied. He seems to
have traversed the whole field of philosophy
in search of truth. His books on ancient and
modern philosophy indicate an amount of

steady, persevering reading through endless volumes which one would think would take all the time in a single lifetime. His work-power was enormous. But then he had splendid health, and he knew how to take care of it. His habits were regular. His domestic life is said, by those who knew it best, to have been singularly happy. He married the sister of John Sterling, the young man of genius whose biography — a very one-sided production — Carlyle wrote; and, a few years after she was removed from this world, a sister of Julius Hare's, another man of literary note, became to Maurice a true helpmeet. These cultured, intelligent, refined women seem to have understood him completely, and his children, one of whom has shown himself a biographer worthy of his eminent father, were real benedictions. Singularly happy in his home, he had, as every original thinker who takes any prominent part in the controversies of his day must have, quite a number of intellectual battles to fight outside. With Candlish, the Scottish divine, as to the extent of the idea of

the divine fatherhood ; with Mansel, the metaphysician, who contended that justice and
mercy in God might be quite something else
than justice and mercy in man — to which
Maurice replied, "Then virtually we have no
God;" with Dr. Jelf, the Principal of King's
College, and some others, Maurice was forced
into controversy; but that was not his spirit
and temper at all.   It was alleged against him
that because he said the word "eternal" as
used in the New Testament (for instance, in
such a passage as this : " This is life eternal,
to know thee, the only true God, and Jesus
Christ whom thou hast sent") meant primar-
ily something profounder than everlasting;
namely, life as it is in God — that his teaching
must necessarily lead to what is called Universalism ; but since the publication of his biography the Universalists have looked upon him
with much less favor than formerly.   One of
his most intimate friends, who knew his mind
most sympathetically, writes : " Maurice says
he cannot see the doctrine of the restoration
of all fallen beings, and thinks that if it be so,

we need a revelation to declare it. He seems
to think (if I understand him rightly) that it
may be possible for a being to exercise his
own free will in resisting God till it becomes
impossible for him to be influenced by any
good." Of course that and similar quotations
dispose of the charge of Universalism. It is
true he refuses to use the word "eternal" as
a synonym for the word "everlasting"; but
that is an entirely different matter.

His life was singularly complete. At
seventy years of age he passed away. Just
before he died he said, "If I may not preach
here, I may preach in other worlds." Throughout his illness he was continually speaking of
sacrifice; of Christ's sacrifice being at the root
of all things. He hardly ever woke in the
night, either in health or when he was sick,
without repeating the Lord's Prayer or the
Benediction, or "Praise God, from whom all
blessings flow."

On the morning on which he died he seemed
to know the end was near; he seemed to make
a great effort to gather himself up, and after

a pause said, slowly and distinctly: "The knowledge of the love of God — the blessing of God Almighty — the Father, the Son, and the Holy Ghost — be amongst you — amongst us — and remain with us forever."·

He never spoke again. In one instant all consciousness was gone. Into the realm of light and love he went — this man, as John Stuart Mill said, who had intellect enough and to spare — this "spiritual splendor," as Gladstone called him — this man whom Kingsley always addressed as "My dear Master"— this man concerning whom the undergraduates of Cambridge said that they always felt better all day for seeing him pass — this man whom servants and poor people whom he visited spoke of as "beautiful," "the angel-faced Maurice," the theological Plato of the nineteenth century.